Higher Still

Finding Eternal Security in Christ

Wellesley Muir

Published by
Amazing Facts, Inc.
PO Box 1058
Roseville, CA 95678-8058
1-800-538-7275

Edited by
Anthony Lester

Cover Design by
Haley Trimmer

Layout by
Greg Solie - Altamont Graphics

ISBN 1-58019-165-7

All Bible Quotations, unless stated otherwise, are from the new King James Version.

Italics not found in original quotations are used for emphasis.

Bold not found in original has been used to create subheadings.

[Brackets] denote supplied words.

Table of Contents

Dedication 7

Message to the Reader 8

1. Go Where you Want to Go 9

2. You've Got to Believe 22

3. The Back of the Bus 37

4. The Greatest Invention 52

5. Eight Ways to Stay Alive 66

6. Fly Your Flag 82

7. Mummy in the Museum 93

8. Too Young? 110

9. Know How to Love 125

10. You Can Be Sure 136

Thank You!

Evelyn, my faithful wife, for reading the manuscript, correcting errors and calling my attention to items needing clarification.

William Fagal, Robert Olson, John Scharffenberg, M. D., and **G. Ralph Thompson** for reading the manuscript and making valuable comments and suggestions.

Terry Nennich, Ronald G. Schmidt and the late **Elmer Walde** for the experience or story you have shared.

Anthony Lester, editor for Amazing Facts, for all you have done to make this book possible.

Youth of the old Inca Union Mission whose interest in reaching heaven inspired me to write this book. All royalties are being donated for youth ministry in Peru.

In Memory

In memory of the late Joe Crews, founder of Amazing Facts. Joe preached and wrote with the fervor of a Bible prophet. He lived to help men, women, and youth find the way to heaven.

Dedication

To my wife, Evelyn. We met in San Francisco. When I finally got the courage to ask, "Will you be willing to go any place in the world with me?" you said, "Yes." Your help in my ministry has been the greatest blessing of my life.

We've been around the world together. God gave us the joy of serving in the Andes, the Amazon, and the Atlantic. After Lake Titicaca, we transferred to the tiny Islands of Bermuda. When our daughters, Gail and Gladys, were ready for college, we moved back to the Central California Conference. Later, we crossed the Pacific to serve in Bangkok, Thailand. Recently we conducted meetings in the Dominican Republic and Nigeria.

Before returning from the Dominican Republic, we took a walk together, hoping to get pictures of the city where we'd been working. The sidewalk narrowed as we walked out on a bridge. I stepped ahead with Evelyn behind. A tall man grabbed the strap on her black shoulder bag and shoved her forward.

I turned to see her face slam into the curb and the mugger running away with her bag. He probably hoped for money. He got an old camera, an umbrella and film with the pictures she had taken of the meetings.

Battered and bruised, broken glasses, bloody wounds, and chipped teeth—but thank the Lord, no broken bones. Someone asked, "Where was your guardian angel?" Evelyn answered, "He was with me all the time. He kept me from being killed." Evelyn believes angels are ready to help you go all the way to the top.

Message for the Reader

Reaching the top is the most important goal of your life. Make it your number one priority.

The testimony of Jesus as found in the writings of Ellen G. White uses the word *ladder* more than 800 times. Check it out for yourself! You will be amazed at what you find. You may wonder why the steps are translated from the Spanish version of *The Acts of the Apostles*. The reason is simple: In Spanish, there is just one word for each step. The same is true with some of the Latin versions of the Bible, but do take time to compare them with the English version.

Following "Points to Remember," you'll find a section titled *Climb Higher*. There you will see an abundance of support for the chapter's content. For the sake of brevity, quotations have been shortened. Please check the original to get the full context.

Pray and ask the Holy Spirit to lead you in climbing still higher. Share what you learn with others. Thank God for the assurance we receive from Jesus.

Chapter 1
Go Where You Want to Go

"Teach me Your way, O Lord ."
—Psalm 27:11

"*M*other!" I glared in anger after washing the dishes at noon. "You're a slave driver. All I do is hoe weeds, carry wood, and wash dishes. The other fellows on this street play all day. You make me work, work, work, and I'm tired of it."

Tears formed in Mother's eyes as I continued. "Cousin Helen told me you're a slave driver, and she's right. I refuse to be your slave any more. I'm leaving home!"

Only eleven years old, I knew exactly where I wanted to go: anywhere, as long as it was as far from home as possible. My parents owned two lots in Paso Robles, California. Our home stood on one, and on the other next to the house, we had a large garden and a grape arbor. Our grapes were the best in the area.

I loved the grapes, and I enjoyed working in the garden until an older cousin, Helen, spent the winter living with my family. Always tearing down whatever my parents said, she planted ideas of rebellion in my young head, not too unlike the devil in the garden. I should have remembered, "There is a way that seems right unto a man, but the end is the way of death" (Proverbs 16:25).

Mother, trying to hide her disappointment, spoke kindly. "I'm sorry you feel like this. Your father and I want you to learn to work and grow up to accomplish worthwhile things."

"I know, Mom," I scowled. "I'm supposed to mow the lawn this afternoon. I've earned money mowing lawns for the neighbors, but I'm not mowing your lawn any more. I'm packing up and leaving."

Instead of a sermon begging me not to run away, Mother smiled. "If you don't like it here, you can go where you want to go."

In the garage, I found an old suitcase and took it to the middle of the living room floor. My younger brother, Don, cried as he watched me pack. My sister Mildred, 16 months younger than I, looked puzzled. My two-year-old baby sister, Shirley, didn't understand what was going on.

Mother brought me an extra pair of pants and a shirt she'd just finished ironing. "You better take these. It may be a while before you earn enough money to buy more clothes."

"Don't worry, Mom. You've taught me to work. I'll get along fine. I just don't want to be your slave anymore."

"Wellesley," she said, "I know you'll want to go to church. Better take your dress shoes and stick in your Bible too."

I'd already packed my suit but forgotten my Sabbath shoes. Mad at God for giving me parents who made me work so much, I'd forgotten all about my Bible. *Mom's right*, I thought. *I'll go get my Bible and Sabbath School Lesson Guide.*

I closed the suitcase and picked it up. *Not too heavy. I'll be able to carry it fine.*

"You won't be seeing me any more," I said, turning to my mother. Mumbling a final "goodbye," I opened the front door, pushed the screen door open, and let it slam behind me. Down the step, across the front porch, I walked on the sidewalk through the lawn I refused to mow. Reaching the white-picket fence, I opened the gate and listened to it creak as I pulled it shut.

On the main sidewalk going past all the homes on the block, I turned left heading north. Reaching the corner, I hesitated. *Should I keep going north?* I ended up turning left and walked to the next corner—Spring Street. I turned left again and walked south to 19th. "Keep going straight ahead?" I asked myself. *No. I'll go left.*

At the next corner, I started south. Half a block away, boys I envied were playing in the street. Halfway across the street I turned 180 degrees and headed north. Suddenly, I saw a familiar-looking white-picket fence. *What am I doing? I'm back in front of my folks' house!* Annoyed, I continued north past my parents' place. At the end of the block, I turned left on 20th Street, walked to Spring Street, and turned left again. At 19th street, I turned left, walked a block, and turned left. I once again looked at the gate in the white-picket fence, but again I kept right on walking past it.

Boy, I thought, this suitcase is really getting heavy! I put the bag down and sat on it. Guess the best thing I can do is start hitchhiking. Before they built a freeway around the town, Spring Street was part of the highway from Los Angeles to San Francisco. According to the signs, San Francisco was 212 miles north and Los Angeles was 212 miles south. *Shall I cross the street and go south or stay on this side and hitchhike north?*

Several cars passed going north. I crossed Spring Street and watched them go by. I nearly decided to try my luck and hold out my thumb. *No, I don't want to go to Los Angeles. I'll go back on the other side of the street and head for San Francisco.*

After watching traffic for a while, I picked up my bag and walked south, got to the corner, turned left, walked to the next corner, and turned left again. In minutes, I stood in front of the gate. My hand trembled when I reached for the lever. *Why am I doing this? I left home forever. Mom won't want me back. She even helped me pack!*

By now I wanted to be home more than anything else. *Mowing the lawn will be more fun than hauling this heavy suitcase around,* I thought. The front door was closed, so I put the suitcase by the front window and sat on it.

Mom was inside. *I'm sure she sees me, but she sure doesn't act like it.* I sat there wondering what to do. It seemed like hours.

I should mow the lawn, but it's late. I'll do it the first thing tomorrow.

Suddenly the door flew open. Mother rushed out and threw her arms around me. "Welcome home! I knew you'd be back. Come on in. Your dad will be home in a few minutes and supper's ready."

I'd talked mean to my mom. *How could she be so nice?* I wondered. Yet I was home! The best place on earth. And food! After hauling the suitcase for 12 city blocks, I felt ravenous. When Dad prayed at evening worship, he thanked the Lord for bringing me home. I prayed silently, "Lord, forgive me. Make me willing to do the work my parents ask me to do. I'll never run away from home again, and I don't want to run away from You."

I've asked thousands of youth, sometimes alone, more often in a group: "If you could go anywhere, where would it be?"

Some answer Hawaii, Alaska, the top of Mount Everest, or even the South Pole. When I lived in Peru, I'd often hear, "the United States." But someone always says heaven. It never fails, and I've been around the world. And everybody else says, "Oh, if that's what you're talking about, heaven is where we really want to go."

So if you had the choice—a classy BMW or fully loaded Mercedes Benz or a really fast Porsche, or eternal life, what would you choose? Everyone says, "We'll take heaven and eternal life."

Why is heaven so attractive? First of all, it means to be with Jesus. The idea of talking to the Creator of the Universe and getting answers to my questions is more exciting than anything else I can think of. I'll ask Him, "Why would You leave heaven and die on a cruel cross just to save me?" And what about living forever with no pain, sickness, or death? No accidents, no broken bones, no funerals.

I can't wait to see the home Jesus is preparing for those who love Him. And God's Word tells us that in the new earth, we will be able to build our own dream home. No monthly payments, no taxes. Ours to enjoy for eternity.

With jet travel today, many of us have seen much of planet earth. Those in God's kingdom will have the opportunity to explore His entire universe. Paul wrote, "Eye has not seen, nor ear heard, nor have entered into the heart of man the things which God has prepared for those who love Him" (1 Corinthians 2:9).

Heaven is where we all want to go, but how can we be sure to get there? At evening family worship, my mother often read Bible stories to her children. One story really grabbed my attention, and it holds part of the answer for getting into heaven.

Jacob and his over-indulgent mother connived to deceive Isaac, his father, and receive the birthright that belonged to his twin brother, Esau.

To deceive his blind and aging father, Jacob wore his brother's best clothes, and his mother placed goatskin on his hands and neck to mimic the feel of the much hairier Esau. Jacob also brought fake venison, though his father had asked Esau to bring real venison. Jacob didn't intend to tell an outright lie, but once with his father, he boldly declared, "I am Esau, your firstborn. I've done just what you requested," though he had not. When his father asked how he hunted down a deer so quickly, Jacob next brought God into the lie: "The Lord Your God brought it to me." When Isaac pressed him, "Are you really my son Esau?" Jacob lied again, saying, "I am."

After discovering Jacob's successful plot, Esau hated his brother because of the stolen blessing and determined, "I will kill Jacob." Jacob's mother warned him of Esau's wrath, and urged him to flee for his life.

Filled with fear, Jacob told his aging parents goodbye and, with only a staff in hand, headed for his uncle's home hundreds of miles away. Though he carried just his staff, a heavy burden of guilt weighed him down.

Now, walking alone through wild country, he avoided meeting others so word of his whereabouts would not get back to his angry brother. *I lied! I lied!*, Jacob kept telling himself. *There's no hope! God will never forgive me!*

By the end of the second day, weary and alone, he began looking for a place to spend the night. If he checked in at a Holiday Inn, his brother would be sure to find him, but there was no Holiday Inn. Not even a Motel 6. Nor did he dare approach some tribal tent to ask for a place to spend the night. Word would quickly reach Esau.

The sun sank slowly behind rugged hills, and darkness crept over the land. With no air mattress or sleeping bag, Jacob lay down on the hard ground. A rock served as his pillow. Plagued by a nagging conscience, Jacob stared into heaven's bright stars.

Hardly daring to pray, he must have whimpered out something like this: "Lord, instead of trusting You, I did my own thing. I tried to buy the birthright. I deceived my father. I lied. Please forgive me before my brother comes and kills me. Please show me You love me!"

Terrifying sounds of wild animals broke the silence of the night. Alone and afraid, yet weary from his long day of walking, Jacob closed his eyes and finally fell asleep.

The God of heaven looked down on the lonely traveler. *This man needs a Savior. I will do something extraordinary for him. I will show him how to be saved.*

Suddenly a dream shocks Jacob. Light, like a thousand lasers, poured down through the night sky. A shining *ladder* touched the earth—its top reaching all the way to heaven. Angels were going up and down this *ladder*, and a melodious voice echoed through the night sky, "I am the Lord God. ... Behold I am with you and will keep you wherever you go" (Genesis 28:13, 15). The vision faded.

The young man woke with a start. "Surely the Lord is in this place and I did not know it" (Genesis 28:16). The next morning, Jacob took the stone used for a pillow and set it up as a monument to the love and grace of God. He called it Bethel, *House of God.*

Jacob could not have asked for more, a promise from the Savior to be with him always. God used a ladder to give Jacob assurance of forgiveness, pardon, and justification. As long as he lived, Jacob retold his vision over and over to family and friends. Its mystery became his lifelong study.

Responding to the Savior's love, he promised, "Of all that You give me, I will surely give a tenth to You" (Genesis 28:22). Feeling the presence of angels, Jacob continued his journey with assurance that God would lead each step of the way. He recognized that salvation is a gift. Now he wanted to give himself to serve the Lord and make progress toward God's kingdom.

Unlike Jacob, I didn't get very far when I ran away from home … only three times around the block. I carried my suitcase less than a mile. My parents didn't ask me to leave, I just ran away from them. Yet like God did with Jacob, they, full of love, took me back.

I even expected a lecture from my dad, but the only mention of the incident he ever made was at worship, when he simply thanked the Lord for sending me home. For me, my parents' love represented the love of Jesus. Their forgiveness, His forgiveness.

I have a problem, along with the rest of the human race. Scripture says, "All our righteousnesses are like filthy rags" (Isaiah 64:6). "All we like sheep have gone astray; We have turned every one to his own way" (Isaiah 53:6). "All have sinned and fall short of the glory of God" (Romans 3:23). "The wages of sin is death" (Romans 6:23).

Our situation gets worse. "Can the Ethiopian change his skin or the leopard its spots? Then may you also do good who are accustomed to do evil" (Jeremiah 13:23). The answer is no. There is absolutely nothing we can do to save ourselves. We desperately need help.

My wife and I live at snow line in the foothills of the Sierra Nevada Mountains. We seldom get snow, but it happens. One unusual year, it snowed eight inches. Followed by even colder weather, the snow turned to ice, staying on for days. When the weather finally warmed, frozen snow on the roof broke off, came crashing down, and tore the side of our chimney.

To make the necessary repair, I needed to get on the roof. I could go out and jump up and down for the rest of my life and I'd never jump high enough to make it. I needed help. I needed a ladder. So I opened the garage door, grabbed the ladder, and leaned it up against the house. It still took effort on my part, but eight steps up the ladder put me on the roof.

The mysterious ladder Jacob saw in his dream is what Christ mentioned when speaking with Nathaniel. "Most assuredly ... you shall see heaven open, and the angels of God ascending and descending upon the Son of Man" (John 1:51). Angels going up and down on the Son of Man? Angels also went up and down on the ladder Jacob saw.

Jesus is the ladder in Jacob's dream! Jesus confirms this, saying, "I am the way, the truth, and the life. No one comes to the Father except through me" (John 14:6). He states further, "Without me, you can do nothing" (John 15:5). I can't get on the roof of our home without a *ladder*. Likewise, I can never get to heaven without Jesus. He's the *ladder!* His amazing love, expressed by His death on the cross, is a powerful magnet drawing you and me to Him.

When I returned home after running away, I had to go through a gate. Jacob, thrilled with the vision of a ladder, exclaimed, "This is the gate of heaven!" (Genesis 28:16, 17). These words of Jesus, then, come as no surprise: "I am the gate. Those who come in through me will be saved." (John 10:9, NLT). Through Jesus, Jacob experienced forgiveness. God opened the gate of heaven to him.

Jacob could look forward with confidence to entrance into heaven. He didn't deserve it, but God gave him this hope anyway. "The Lamb slain from the foundation of the world" (Revelation 13:8), bridged the gap made by his sin.

Yet God does not leave us standing at the gate with the right to enter heaven with our lives unchanged. We come to Jesus just as we are, but He doesn't leave us that way. Without change, we would not be fit for companionship with God and the angels! Jesus is the ladder to transformation. In mercy, He offers His grace, His power, to live a changed life. Through clinging to Jesus, the ladder let down from heaven, and by climbing with Him, we are changed to be like Him.

Referring to the Savior, Peter says, "His divine power has given to us all things that pertain to life and godliness" (2 Peter 1:3). Salvation is a gift from God. Jesus paid the price on the cross. Because of what Jesus has done for us, we are admonished to "be even more diligent to make our calling and election sure" (2 Peter 1:10).

Jesus is the gate, the door, to heaven. In Him we find forgiveness, *justification*. Jesus is also a ladder. By climbing with Him we are transformed, *sanctified*, restored to the image of God. Forgiveness and transformation are both God's work. It's our privilege to co-operate with Christ in this endeavor, and we should not resist Him. It's our choice to let the Holy Spirit work in us.

Ladders have steps. Jesus even inspired Peter to share eight steps on the ladder of progress that takes us to heaven. He presents heaven's plan for the development of Christian character saying, "Add to your faith, virtue, to virtue science, to science temperance, to temperance patience, to patience piety, to piety fraternity, to fraternity love" (2 Peter 1:5-7, author's translation). This is the ladder of true sanctification. Here we learn to walk in the footsteps of Jesus.

Of course, Christ is more than a ladder; He's a climbing companion. As a ladder, He provides support for my journey from earth to heaven. Jesus promised, "I am with you always" (Matthew 28:20). This means I don't have to do it by myself. I can climb with Him. He is with me every step of the way.

Where do you want to go? The best place in the universe is heaven. I was an 11-year-old rebel, convicted of sin for breaking the fifth commandment, "Honor your father and your mother," when I suddenly realized my need for a Savior. More than anything else, I wanted to go to heaven. How can I be absolutely sure how to get there?

The ladder is a symbol of the way. Like Jacob seeing the ladder let down from heaven, I know that Jesus is my only hope of getting to heaven. The cross symbolizes the cost. The Savior's death on the cross joins me to God.

I've learned, however, Jesus is not an escalator. You don't just jump on for a free ride. Jesus is a *ladder*. Ladders are made to climb. We can go all the way to heaven by climbing with Him—this is what Peter wrote about. We will begin exploring these steps to heaven in the next chapter. The Savior promises, "If anyone enters by Me, he will be saved" (John 10:9).

"Jesus is the WAY to heaven,
I will climb with Him."

Points to Remember

1. Because of sin, we all face the death penalty and need a Savior.
2. Salvation is deliverance from the power and effects of sin (See Webster's Collegiate Dictionary).
3. We cannot save ourselves.
4. We need a ladder.
5. Jesus is the ladder. He is the only way to heaven. He wants to be our climbing companion.
6. Jesus' love, revealed at the cross draws us to Him.
7. Only Jesus can forgive our sins and make us right with God.

Climb Higher

God's Offer: The Ladder to Heaven

"Jacob … dreamed, and behold, a *ladder* was set up on the earth, and its top reached to heaven; and there the angels of God were ascending and descending on it" (Genesis 28:10, 12).

"You shall see heaven open, and the angels of God ascending and descending upon the Son of Man" (John 1:51).

"Trusting God implicitly, you will recognize **the voice of Jesus saying: 'Come up higher'**" (Testimonies for the Church, 6:48).

"**The Son of God** … is the ladder by which we are to ascend to God" (Martin Luther, *Christianity Today*, December 9, 1988).

Jesus Is the Ladder

"**The *ladder* represented Christ;** He is the channel of communication between heaven and earth. … The words of Christ to Nathanael were in harmony with the figure of [Jacob's] *ladder*. … Here the Redeemer identifies Himself as the mystic *ladder*" (*Review and Herald*, November 11, 1890).

"Our Saviour is the ladder which Jacob saw. ... If any of us are finally saved, it will be by clinging to Jesus as to the rounds of a ladder. To the believer, Christ is made wisdom and righteousness, sanctification and redemption" (*Testimonies for the Church*, 5:539).

"I have found a sure rule for success in the Christian journey ... in 2 Peter 1:5-7. We must climb this *ladder*, round after round, remembering that God is above it, ready to help us in our efforts. ... Let us begin today to climb ... never looking back; for we have the word of the inspired apostle that if we do these things we shall never fall." (*Signs of the Times*, October 22, 1885).

"The representation given to Jacob of a ladder ... is a representation of the plan of salvation" (*Signs of the Times*, April 11, 1895).

How to Climb Higher

"Through Christ you may climb the ladder of progress, and bring every power under the control of Jesus. ... In spirit, in thought, in word, and in action, you may make manifest that you are moved by the Spirit of Christ" (*Sons and Daughters of God*, 118).

"He who is being sanctified . . . will follow in the footsteps of Christ until grace is lost in glory. The righteousness by which we are **justified** is imputed; the righteousness by which we are sanctified is imparted. The first is our title to heaven, the second is our fitness for heaven" (*Messages to Young People*, 35).

"Our title to heaven and our fitness for it are found in the righteousness of Christ. The Lord can do nothing toward the recovery of man until, convinced of his own weakness, and stripped of all self-sufficiency, he yields himself to the control of God. Then he can receive the gift that God is waiting to bestow" (*The Desire of Ages*, 300).

"Break down every barrier and let the Saviour into your heart. Let self die. Surrender your will and die to self now, just now, and leave God to make your way for you" (*This Day with God*, 323).

Why Climb the Ladder? Heaven Is Where You Want to Go

"In My Father's house are many mansions; if it were not so, I would have told you. I go to prepare a place for you. And if I go and prepare a place for you, I will come again and receive you to Myself; that where I am, *there* you may be also" (John 14:2, 3).

"God will wipe away every tear from their eyes; there shall be no more death, nor sorrow, nor crying. There shall be no more pain, for the former things have passed away'" (Revelation 21:4).

" 'They shall build houses and inhabit them; they shall plant vineyards and eat their fruit. They shall not build and another inhabit; they shall not plant and another eat; for as the days of a tree, so shall be the days of My people, and My elect shall long enjoy the work of their hands. They shall not labor in vain. . . . The wolf and the lamb shall feed together, the lion shall eat straw like the ox, and dust shall be the serpent's food. They shall not hurt nor destroy in all My holy mountain,' says the Lord" (Isaiah 65:21-23, 25).

"Human language is inadequate to describe the reward of the righteous. It will be known only to those who behold it. No finite mind can comprehend the glory of the Paradise of God" (*The Great Controversy*, 674).

"Point the youth to Peter's ladder of eight rounds ... and with earnest solicitation urge them to climb to the very top" (*Maranatha*, 84).

Chapter 2
You've Got to Believe

Jesus affirms, *"I am the WAY, the truth and the life.*
No one comes to the Father except through me."
—John 14:6

So we are saved by climbing with Jesus,
and the first step on the ladder is FAITH.

*W*e lived in Bermuda when a successful airline jingle grabbed my attention: "Go where you want to go! You've gotta believe!" Of course, it takes faith to climb into a jumbo jet and fly more than 800 miles over the Atlantic. You've got to believe the equipment is properly maintained. You've got to trust the pilot. Believe me, I know. I've made that flight many times. And flights over the Pacific from Los Angeles to Bangkok later tested my *faith* in airlines even more.

Now, let me test your *faith*. Imagine you are here with me right now. I have something in my pocket I've never seen. You've never seen it either. In fact, no one has ever seen it! But I'm going to take it out of my pocket and show it to you. After I show it to you, I'll never see it again. You'll never see it again. No one will ever see it again.

Do you believe me?

I've asked this question to young people around the world, and it's about impossible to get anyone to raise a hand to say they believe.

So what do I do? I reach in my pocket and pull out an unshelled peanut and shake it. The noise tells everyone there's something inside. I then break it open and hold up a peanut.

Have I ever seen this before? No! Have you ever seen it before? No! Has anyone ever seen it before? No!

I stick the peanut in my mouth and start chewing. I swallow it and ask, "Will anyone ever see that peanut again?" Everyone smiles. It's easy to say we have a lot of *faith*, but the truth is—all of us need more *faith*.

Long before Jacob dreamed of the ladder, his 99-year-old grandfather, Abraham, received a visit from the Lord. God said something like this: "You were 75 years old when I promised, 'In you all the families of the earth shall be blessed.' Standing together under a night sky, I asked you to look toward heaven and count the stars. 'I can't do it,' you said. I responded, 'You won't be able to count your descendants either.' You believed and I accounted it to you for righteousness."

Abraham recalled, *10 years passed and no promised son. At 85, I began to doubt. My faith vanished, so I followed Sarah's suggestion in an attempt to do what You promised to do.*

The father of righteousness by faith bore a son by works. *My works*, Abraham remembered, *resulted in a boy born to an Egyptian woman named Hagar.* Abraham listened as God continued speaking. "I will bless Sarah and give you a son."

"Lord, you've got to be kidding!" Abraham fell on his face and laughed. *"Shall a child be born to a man who is one hundred years old? And shall Sarah, who is ninety years old, bear a child?"* (Genesis 17:17).

The next time God visited Abraham's tent, Sarah also laughed at His promise. *"Shall I surely bear a child since I am old?"* (Genesis 18:13). She needed to learn that there is nothing too hard for the Lord.

Indeed, a year later, Abraham, 100 years old, and his wife Sarah, 91, rejoiced at the birth of a son, Isaac. Our God is able—you've got to believe. We need *faith*!

Abraham's *faith* faltered when he fathered Ishmael, but at 120 years of age, his *faith* was challenged by a new test. Isaac, a handsome young man, was 20 and a joy to his aging parents. "Abraham," God called. "Take now your son, your only son

Isaac, whom you love, and go to the land of Moriah, and offer him there as a burnt offering" (Genesis 22:1, 2).

Troubled thoughts flooded the old man's mind. *I can't do that! God's law tells us not to kill. I'm under an illusion, for God wouldn't ask me to do this. It will kill Sarah—she lives for her son. Sacrificing Isaac will make it impossible for God to fulfill His promise that all nations of the earth will be blessed through me!*

Abraham wanted to wake Sarah and tell her of God's command. *I can't do that,* he reasoned. *She'll try to talk me out of it.* As he struggled in the darkness of the night, the voice of God kept echoing in his ears. "Take your son; offer him!"

Sometime before dawn, Abraham awakened Isaac. "God has told me to go to Mount Moriah and offer a sacrifice. Son, I want you to go with me."

Isaac had joined his father in sacrificing on other occasions and counted it a privilege. "Yes, father," he jumped up. "I'll get ready." They saddled a donkey, took wood, and asked two of Abraham's young men to go along.

All through the long day, father and son walked together. Isaac, seeing his father's unusual silence must have wondered, *What's troubling my father? He's always been happy to have me with him. Now he acts like we're on our way to a funeral.*

Every time Abraham looked at Isaac, he thought of Sarah. *The knife I'll use to kill my son will pierce her heart too. Isaac's so loving and obedient, how can I do this to him?*

It seemed like the longest day of his life. When night finally came, they set up camp. Isaac and the young men quickly fell asleep. Abraham, hoping for some heavenly messenger to appear and tell him to take the boy unharmed back to his mother, spent the night in prayer.

All the next day, Abraham agonized. "Why Lord? Why are you asking me to take the life of my heir?" The strange command that would leave him and Sarah childless rang constantly in his ears. On the morning of the third day, father and son got their first glimpse of Mount Moriah. Abraham turned to the young men. "You fellows can stay here with the donkey. Isaac and I will go on and worship our God. We'll be back later." We? … Abraham knew he'd be coming back alone. Word would soon get around that he had murdered his son.

Isaac carried the wood on his back. Abraham took the fire and a knife. The son looked at his father. "We have fire and wood. Where's the lamb?"

"No problem, Son. God will provide."

Reaching Mount Moriah, they built an altar and arranged the wood. "Isaac, my son," Abraham said at last. "You are a miracle child—a gift from God for your mother and me in our old age. I don't understand. God spoke to me and asked me to come and sacrifice you on this mountain."

The muscular young man could have turned on his old father or simply run away. From a child, he had been taught to obey. "Father," he said, "If this is the will of God, I'm ready."

Abraham hugged his boy one last time, bound him, and placed him over the wood on the altar. He must have prayed, "Lord, I'm doing what you asked me to do. Please come and raise my son from the dead."

With a shaking hand, Abraham held the knife high, ready to take the life of Isaac. "Abraham, stop!" The Angel of the Lord called from heaven. "Do not slay your son! It's enough. You have not held back your only son. Now I know you truly have *faith* in God."

Looking behind him, Abraham saw a ram caught in the bushes. "So Abraham went and took the ram, and offered it up for a burnt offering instead of his son" (Genesis 22:13). The Angel of the Lord declared, "In your seed all the nations of the earth shall be blessed, because you have obeyed My voice" (Genesis 22:18). Scripture says, "By *faith* Abraham, when he was tested, offered up Isaac" (Hebrews 11:17).

What did *faith* do for Abraham? "By *faith* Abraham obeyed" (Hebrews 11:8). He and the other faithful mentioned by Paul in his letter to the Hebrews, "died in faith, not having received the promises, but having seen them afar off were assured of them, embraced them and confessed that they were strangers and pilgrims on the earth. For those who say such things declare plainly that they seek a homeland … a heavenly *country.* Therefore God ... has prepared a city for them" (Hebrews 11:13, 14, 16).

It's important to remember that God preached the gospel of Jesus to Abraham. The ram offered in place of Isaac represents Jesus, the Lamb of God, who died as a sacrifice for our sins.

God wants us to remember that "the gospel of Christ ... is the power of God to salvation for everyone who believes. ... In it the righteousness of God is revealed from *faith* to *faith*; as it is written, *'The just shall live by faith'*" (Romans 1:16, 17).

Faith in Jesus brings salvation. *Faith* is the first step on the *ladder* to heaven. Your prayer, my prayer, like that of the apostles should always be, "Lord, 'Increase our *faith*'" (Luke 17:5).

Webster's Collegiate Dictionary definitions for *faith* help us understand our need:

1. Allegiance to duty or a person.
2. Belief and trust in and loyalty to God.
3. Complete trust.
4. Firm belief in something for which there is no proof.

Paul describes *faith* as "the substance of things hoped for, the evidence of things not seen" (Hebrews 11:1). He continues, "By *faith* we understand that the worlds were framed by the word of God" (Hebrews 11:3).

The very first verse in the Bible says, "In the beginning, God created the heavens and the earth" (Genesis 1:1). "Then God said, 'Let Us make man in Our image, according to Our likeness; ... So God created man in His own image ... male and female He created them" (Genesis 1:26, 27).

Do you believe in a Creator? Look at yourself in a mirror. You see the evidence. The complex design of the human body is awesome. Think about the abilities of the human eye. Check out your hands. How about your heart? Every part of your body down to the smallest cell functions in perfect harmony. Jesus is our Creator. I believe it based on evidence.

Let me tell you a story. You decide if it's a fabrication. Fifty million years ago, an explosion occurred in outer space. Cooling gasses congealed into pieces of metal and glass. Turning into asteroids, they sped across the cosmos. Vaporized by heat built up from friction on entering earth's atmosphere at astronomical velocities, they tumbled across the sky like shooting stars.

The strange objects from space cooled down and landed in an Arizona desert. Millions of years passed. Erosion caused one piece of glass to form a crystal. A piece of metal turned into a stainless steel case. More metal formed a stainless steel band. There was a tiny piece of quartz. Oh, and some hands.

All of these pieces were scattered around the desert for hundreds of thousands of years. One day a whirlwind picked them up and spun them around. They all came together forming a watch so accurate it only gains about 10 seconds a year.

Great! But it's not true. I look at my watch. It says, "Swiss Made." I've never been to the factory. I've never seen the watchmaker. But you know he exists, and I know he exists. I have the evidence on my wrist right now. I have *faith* to believe in a watchmaker I've never seen. So do you.

God is the Creator of our complex universe. You and I are the evidence. I have *faith* to believe He created our planet with its solar system in six days just like He said.

The stars, the sun, the moon, dry land, ocean, plants, animals, birds, fish. All are evidence of a God who designed the universe, our world, and everything in it, including you and me. It is even necessary to believe in His creation to truly understand salvation.

Faith is necessary for those who want to reach the top of the *ladder.* "Without *faith* it is impossible to please Him, for he who comes to God must believe that He is, and that He is a rewarder of those who diligently seek Him" (Hebrews 11:6). "Whatever is not of *faith* is sin" (Romans 14:23, KJV).

One of the best ways to increase *faith* is by prayerfully reading the Bible. "*Faith* comes by hearing, and hearing by the word of God" (Romans 10:17).

Faith is a gift. "For by grace you have been saved through *faith*, and that not of yourselves; it is the gift of God" (Ephesians 2:8). "God has dealt to each one a measure of *faith*" (Romans 12:3). This marvelous gift comes from Christ. We must be constantly, "Looking unto Jesus, the author and finisher of our *faith*" (Hebrews 12:2).

Jesus spoke to Paul saying, "I now send you … to turn *them* from darkness to light, and *from* the power of Satan to God, that they may receive forgiveness of sins and an inheritance among those who are sanctified by *faith* in Me" (Acts 26:17, 18).

Faith delivers us from the power of darkness. *Faith* brings forgiveness of sins. *Faith* in Jesus brings grace with power to live holy lives in preparation for a home in heaven.

Only weeks after experiencing forgiveness when my parents let me come home even after declaring, "I'm leaving forever," I tossed and turned in bed unable to sleep. In bed before eight o'clock, I was still awake at midnight. I wanted to pray. *No*, I thought. *God won't listen to me.* Several times I sat up in bed. I rolled over. I got out of bed and stood up. I got back in bed, put my head on the pillow and sobbed.

My mother came into the room and turned on the light. "What's the matter? Are you sick?"

"No, I'm not sick."

Mom looked at her watch. "Wellesley, it's 2:00 a.m. You need to sleep."

"I want to, but I can't."

My mother sat on the bed and put her arm around me. I cried. "Tell me what's wrong," she said. "I can tell something's bothering you."

I finally blurted out, "Mom, I'm a thief, and God can't forgive me."

"A thief! What do you mean you're a thief? Jesus forgave the thief on the cross. He can forgive you."

I sat up and looked at my mother. "School got out early. You thought I spent the afternoon at the library. I didn't. I talked Robert into going to the river with me. We stole some old lumber from George Bell's farm and built a raft. The river's full and we had fun using poles to paddle around. I've always wanted a boat."

Alarmed, my mother said, "Don't you know you could fall off the raft and drown?"

"I know how to swim so you don't need to worry," I replied. "The problem is I stole the lumber. How can God forgive me?"

"You've got to believe!" Mother said. "The Bible says, 'Believe on the Lord Jesus Christ, and you will be saved.' Jesus invites us to believe, repent, confess, forsake sin and love and obey Him. My mom took my Bible off the dresser and began to read. "If we confess our sins, He is faithful and just to forgive our sins" (1 John 1:9). Why don't you ask Jesus right now to forgive you for stealing lumber?"

I took a handkerchief, dried my tears, climbed out of bed, knelt down, and buried my face in Mother's lap. She smiled when I finished asking God for forgiveness. "You must always have *faith* to believe that 'the blood of Jesus Christ ... cleanses us from all sin' (1 John 1:7). You asked Jesus to forgive you. Now you need to return the lumber. The Holy Spirit leads us to repent and confess. After asking Jesus to forgive our sins, we also need to do everything possible to make things right."

"I will, Mom. I promise."

I climbed back into bed. Mom gave me a kiss, turned out the light and left. I closed my eyes and the next thing I knew my folks were calling me for breakfast. The minute school let out, I ran to the river. Thankful for 'the precious blood of Jesus,' I began taking the raft apart. The joy of forgiveness flooded my young heart as I raced home to report the stolen lumber had been returned.

Soon after I turned 13, two young preachers came and pitched a big tent on a vacant lot only blocks from my home. I attended their meetings every night. All they said about *faith* in Jesus and the Bible made sense. Grateful for God's grace and forgiveness, I chose to place my faith in Jesus and prepare for baptism in the name of the Father, the Son, and the Holy Spirit.

Lawrence Nelson conducted a baptismal class every Thursday at the church school I attended. He taught us to honor Jesus by turning away from the things of the world. He showed from the Bible that before baptism, we need to confess every sin. The Holy Spirit worked on my conscience. "You've got something else to make right."

So I went to my parents. "You've taught me to honor Jesus and fill my mind with good things. You taught me not to read funny papers. Please forgive me because I've been hiding the funny paper in the wood box and reading it when you aren't looking. I've asked Jesus to help me not do this any more." With that confession, a big burden rolled away.

God's Word declares, "He who believes [has *faith*] and is baptized will be saved; but he who does not believe will be condemned" (Mark 16:16). Jesus presents only two ways. Have *faith* and be saved. Fail to believe and be lost. I've learned that the Bible only recognizes faith which leads to obedience and true obedience always results from faith.

My decision to follow Christ filled my heart with joy. "For as many of you as were baptized into Christ have put on Christ' (Galatians 3:27). I look back on my baptism as the most important event in my life. I didn't want to run away from home anymore. I would never think of running away from God. I wanted to go to heaven.

A *ladder* provides a way up. A public profession of *faith* in Jesus by baptism is placing your feet on the first rung of the *ladder*, yet it serves no purpose unless you climb. Jesus' death on the cross cannot save unless we accept His gift of salvation. Through *faith* in Him, we can overcome by "the blood of the Lamb." The Christian life is one of constant progress.

Living for Jesus is like climbing a *ladder*. You'll never get to the top unless you keep climbing. Thomas Huxley had it right when he wrote in *Reader's Digest*: "The rung of a *ladder* was never meant to rest upon, but only to hold a man's foot long enough to put the other somewhat higher." The two young preachers in the big tent taught me to aim high. *Faith* is the first step. I must constantly cling to Christ and climb.

Jesus is the *ladder* to heaven and He gave me a new challenge: "Pursue righteousness, godliness, *faith*, love, patience, gentleness. Fight the good fight of *faith*, lay hold on eternal life" (1 Timothy 6:11, 12). "For we through the Spirit eagerly wait for the hope of righteousness by *faith*" (Galatians 5:5).

You won't see the words very often, but righteousness by *faith* is what this book is about. Paul quotes Jesus as saying, "That they may receive forgiveness of sins and an inheritance among those who are sanctified by *faith* in Me" (Acts 26:18). Paul wrote: "We have received grace and apostleship for obedience to the *faith*" (Romans 1:5). James explains, "*Faith* without works is dead" (James 2:26).

Through *faith* I accept the righteousness of Christ. Jesus gives me strength to do His will. Paul assures us, "I can do all things through Christ who strengthens me" (Philippians 4:13). Jesus is the ladder. I can climb with Him. John writes, "This is the victory that has overcome the world—our *faith*" (1 John 5:4). *Faith* in Jesus brings salvation.

Jesus is the *ladder*. He says, "I am the way, the truth, and the life. No ones comes to the Father except through me" (John 14:6). I must pray every day, "Show me now Your way, that I may know You and that I may find grace in Your sight" (Exodus 33:13).

Climbing with Jesus, we will be able to say, "I have fought the good fight, I have finished the race, I have kept the *faith*. Finally, there is laid up for me the crown of righteousness, which the Lord the righteous Judge, will give to me on that Day, and not to me only but also to all who have loved His appearing" (2 Timothy 4:7, 8).

FAITH in Jesus brings salvation,
Lord, increase our FAITH!

Points to Remember
1. *Faith* is a gift of God. It includes belief, trust, and commitment.
2. *Faith* leads to repentance, confession, and a new life in Christ—we call this conversion.
3. *Faith* in Jesus brings pardon or forgiveness for past sin—we call this justification.
4. We are sanctified by *faith*. Grace and the Holy Spirit provide power to live a life of victory.
5. *Faith* is perfect trust in God followed by obedience to His commands.
6. *Faith* leads to obedience. Obedience results from *faith*.
7. Baptism is a public testimony of our *faith* in Jesus.
8. Heaven's joy fills our hearts as we prepare to spend eternity with the Savior.

Climb Higher

God Offers Faith

"Reach up, higher and still higher, taking hold of one line of *faith* after another" (*That I May Know Him*, 328).

"Look up, look up, and let your *faith* continually increase" (*Prophets and Kings*, 732).

"*Faith* [is one of] the rounds of the ladder. We are saved by climbing round after round, mounting step after step, to the height of Christ's ideal for us" (Translated from *Los Hechos de los Apostoles*, 422. Compare with *The Acts of the Apostles*, 530).

The Ladder

"Teach me Your way, O Lord; I will walk in Your truth" (Psalm 86:11).

"Jesus says, 'I am the way, ... I am that *ladder* which Jacob saw, the base of it resting firmly upon the earth, while the topmost round reaches to the throne of God. I am the light that shines upon every soul who climbs up by me. I am the life, inspiring with *faith* and love as you move onward and upward'" (Ellen G. White, *Review and Herald*, April 12, 1892).

"**Take the first step**, and the next step on the *ladder* of progress will be easier. The *ladder* ... must be climbed round by round. ... God is above the ladder, and His glory will illuminate every step. ... The path of *faith* and self-denial is an upward path; its way is heavenward, and as you advance, the misleading clouds of doubt and evil will be left behind" (*Review and Herald*, October 9, 1894).

"**True, saving faith** is a precious treasure of inestimable value. It is not superficial. The just lives by *faith* a truly spiritual, Christlike life. It is through *faith* that the steps are taken one at a time up the *ladder*" (*Our High Calling*, 67).

The Step of Faith

"Without *faith* it is impossible to please Him" (Heb. 11:6).

"**Faith is the spiritual hand** that touches infinity" (*Testimonies for the Church*, 6:467).

"*Faith* **is rendering to God the intellectual powers**, abandonment of the mind and will to God, and making Christ the only door to enter into the kingdom of heaven" (*Faith and Works*, 25).

"**Our *faith* must rest upon evidence, not demonstration**. ... Those who really desire to know the truth will find plenty of evidence on which to rest their *faith*" (*Steps to Christ*, 105).

Faith Leads to Repentance, Baptism, and a New Life

"Repent, and be baptized ... in the name of Jesus Christ for the forgiveness of your sins; and you shall receive the gift of the Holy Spirit" (Acts 2:38, RSV).

"He who covers his sins will not prosper, but whoever confesses and forsakes them will have mercy" (Proverbs 28:13).

"Buried with Him in baptism ... you also were raised with Him through *faith*" (Colossians 2:12).

"Just as Christ was raised from the dead by the glory of the Father, even so we also should walk in newness of life ... that we should no longer be slaves of sin" (Romans 6:4, 6).

Saved by Faith

"Be not slothful, but followers of them who through faith and patience inherit the promises" (Hebrews 6:12).

"**Faith is the condition** upon which God has seen fit to promise pardon to sinners" (*Selected Messages*, 1:366).

"**Salvation** is through faith in Jesus Christ alone" (*Faith and Works*, 18).

"**When you respond to the drawing of Christ**, and join yourself to Him, you manifest saving faith" (*God's Amazing Grace*, 183).

Faith Works

"What does it profit ... if someone says he has *faith* but does not have works? Can *faith* save him? ... *Faith* without works is dead. ... A man is justified by works, and not by *faith* only" (James 2:14, 20, 24).

"The Holy Scriptures ... are able to make you wise for salvation through *faith* which is in Christ Jesus" (2 Timothy 3:15).

"**By obedience the people were to give evidence of their faith.** So all who hope to be saved by the merits of the blood of Christ should realize that they themselves have something to do in securing their salvation. While it is Christ only that can redeem us from the penalty of transgression, we are to turn from sin to obedience. Man is to be saved by *faith*, not by works; yet his *faith* must be shown by his works" (*Patriarchs and Prophets*, 279).

"**The desire for an easy religion** that requires no striving, no self-denial, no divorce from the follies of the world, has made the doctrine of *faith*, and *faith* only, a popular doctrine. ... The testimony of the word of God is against this ensnaring doctrine of *faith* without works. It is not faith that claims the favor of Heaven without complying with the conditions upon which mercy is to be granted, it is presumption; for genuine *faith* has its foundation in the promises and provisions of the Scriptures" (*The Great Controversy*, 472).

Righteousness by Faith

"The righteousness of God ... is through *faith* in Jesus Christ to all ... who believe" (Romans 3:22).

"**Justification is a full, complete pardon of sin**. The moment a sinner accepts Christ by *faith*, that moment he is pardoned. The righteousness of Christ is imputed to him, and he is no more to doubt God's forgiving grace" (*The Faith I Live By*, 107).

"**Yes, we are justified by faith alone**, but the faith that justifies is never alone. ... We are justified by faith, a faith that is active in love leading to holiness" (Timothy George, "A Call to Freedom," *Decision*, April 2001).

"**It is the righteousness of Christ**, His own unblemished character, that through *faith* is imparted to all who receive Him as their personal Saviour" (*Christ's Object Lessons*, 31).

The Faith of Jesus

"Here are those who keep the commandments of God and the *faith* of Jesus" (Revelation 14:12).

"*Faith* in the ability of Christ to save us amply and fully and entirely is the *faith* of Jesus" (*Selected Messages*, 3:172).

"**The *faith* of Jesus** takes in the whole life and divine character of Christ" (*Manuscript Releases*, 224).

"**Keep in mind** the . . . thought of the Lord's soon return. . . . Through the aid of the Holy Spirit we are to resist natural inclinations and tendencies to wrong, and weed out of the life every un-Christlike element. Thus we shall prepare our hearts for the reception of God's blessing, which will impart to us grace and bring us into harmony with the *faith* of Jesus" (*In Heavenly Places*, 347).

Victory Through Faith

"For whatever is born of God overcomes the world. And this is the victory that has overcome the world—our *faith*" (1 John 5:4).

"Taking the shield of *faith* . . . you will be able to quench all the fiery darts of the wicked one" (Ephesians 6:16).

"**God works for the striving ones** who exercise *faith* and practice godliness in the home life, in the church life, and in the small and larger interests that will unfold as we advance upward, climbing on the *ladder* that Peter has presented to every believer" (*Manuscript Releases*, 5:341)

Assurance of Faith

"These all died in *faith*, not having received the promises, but having seen them afar off were assured of them" (Hebrews 11:13).

Chapter 3
The Back of the Bus

Jesus proclaims, *"I am the WAY, the truth and the life.*
No one comes to the Father except through me."
—John 14:6

We are saved by climbing with Jesus.
Steps up the *ladder* include faith and VIRTUE.

For days I paddled up river with a Campa Indian guide in a dugout canoe. Restless nights trying to sleep on the floor under a mosquito net followed long hours perspiring under the tropical sun in the Upper Amazon Jungle of Peru.

Each night we spoke to tribal people, sharing our faith in Jesus and His promise to come soon and take us to our heavenly home. Exhausted after the last meeting, I began thinking about my wife and daughters at mission headquarters on the other side of the Andes. Anxious to see my family, I prayed, "Lord, if it's Your will, help me get home tomorrow."

Impossible, I thought. *It takes at least three days to get to Lima. Why am I asking God for something that can't happen?*

But you've been telling people about the ladder to heaven. Where's your faith?

Juan Ucayali, my guide, would stay and continue instructing new Christians. Another Indian believer with a dugout canoe offered to take me to the Nevati mission station.

Leaving before sunrise, we paddled through rapids down the swift river reaching Nevati just as a canoe with an outboard motor was leaving for Puerto Bermudez. I paid the fare and leaped on board. An air taxi landed just as we arrived at

Puerto Bermudez. I ran and bought a ticket for the last available seat.

The Cessna roared off a dirt runway and I looked down at dense green jungle. *It does look like God is doing something special for me today,* I thought, *but I'll probably have to spend the night in San Ramón since all buses leave early in the morning.* The plane landed, and I jumped out. A *colectivo* (a car that carries passengers like a bus), with one empty seat waited, ready to leave for La Oroya near the highest pass in the Andes.

"I'll take it," I called to the driver. He tied my suitcase on top and covered it with plastic. *Incredible! God is so good.* Hours later, the *colectivo* pulled to a stop in La Oroya. A bus across the street had its engine running ready to leave. I grabbed my luggage and ran. The bus driver said, "We're going to Lima right now. There's only one seat left, and it's in the very back."

"No problem," I said and paid for the ticket.

My seat in the back row was in the middle, the most uncomfortable seat on the bus. Two men sat on my right, a young man on my left and next to him a girl in her late teens. The two started flirting. Before long they were holding hands. Soon he had his arm around her.

"Do you like to dance?" he asked. "What kind of music do you like?" While crossing the highest pass at Ticlio at over 16,000 feet, he kissed the girl and asked, "Do you believe in love at first sight?"

"I think so," she said, "but I'm not quite sure. It depends."

The bus swung passengers from one side to the other as it raced around curves going down to the coast of Peru. My seatmate, holding the girl tight, blurted out, "Will you marry me?"

Nothing bashful about this couple, I thought!

During the long ride, this young man surprised me by speaking in English, which the girl did not understand. He said, "I had a date with another girl tonight, but she is boring, so without telling her, I decided to take a bus to Lima and have some fun."

He had recently graduated from school in the United States and landed a job as a mining engineer in Peru. We were on the outskirts of Lima when the young man kissed the girl again and said, "Let's get married tonight."

The bus pulled into the station. Passengers in the back of the bus were the last to get out. I watched the girl climb into a taxi with the engineer. They headed for a hotel where they would spend the rest of the night together.

A taxi took me to our apartment near the Inca Union Mission headquarters. Amazing! Out of one of the most remote spots in the Amazon Jungle and over the Andes to my home in Lima all in one day. *I can hardly believe it.* "Lord," I prayed. "Thank you for increasing my faith."

Faith! Faith's the first step on the *ladder*. The second step is *virtue*. *Virtue* is not what I witnessed in the conduct of the young mining engineer in the back of the bus. It's vice. It's not love; it's lust. The book of Genesis refers to it as "great wickedness and sin against God." It's breaking the seventh commandment.

All of us who want to live in heaven with Jesus need to ask ourselves, "Are we just looking for a good time, or do we want to please our Savior and do His will?"

You want to get to the top of the *ladder*. You want to live in heaven with Jesus. Look at these words written by a fisherman: "Blessed be the God and Father of our Lord Jesus Christ, who according to His abundant mercy has begotten us again to a living hope through the resurrection of Jesus Christ from the dead, to an inheritance incorruptible and undefiled and that does not fade away, *reserved in heaven for you*" (1 Peter 1:3, 4).

Jesus is the *ladder*. He has an inheritance reserved in heaven for you. To be an heir of the kingdom, we must climb with Jesus. He says, "I am the *WAY*, the truth and the life" (John 14:6).

Peter writes, "To those who have obtained like precious faith with us by the righteousness of our God and Savior Jesus Christ ... as His divine power has given to us all things that pertain to life and godliness, through the knowledge of Him who called us by glory and *virtue,* by which have been given to us exceedingly great and precious promises, that through these you may be partakers of the divine nature, having escaped the corruption that is in the world through lust" (2 Peter 1:1, 3, 4).

All who have faith in Jesus are called "by glory and *virtue.*" *Virtue* is the result of escaping the corruption of lust that is in the world. Paul describes lust as a work of the flesh including, "adultery, fornication, uncleanness, lewdness" (Galatians 5:19). He quickly adds, "Those who practice such things will not inherit the kingdom of God" (Galatians 5:21). *Virtue* leads us to avoid sexual immorality, impure thoughts, and lustful pleasure.

Jesus taught that conditions in the world before His coming would be like those in the time of Noah. "Then the Lord saw that the wickedness of man was great in the earth, and that every intent of the thoughts of his heart was only evil continually" (Genesis 6:5).

We live in a world of vice, but Jesus calls us to live lives of *virtue.* Let's check some of Webster's definitions for three important words:

1. Virgin: "free of impurity or stain"; "a person who has not had sexual intercourse."
2. *Virtue*: "conformity to a standard of right"; "moral excellence"
3. Victory: "overcoming"; "success in a struggle against difficulties."

Climbing with Jesus we become free of the impurity of sin. He gives us power to conform to His standard of *virtue.* With Christ there is victory. He "is able to keep you from falling" (Jude 24, KJV).

Joseph, a handsome teenager, served an officer of Pharaoh. Scripture says, "The Lord made all he did to prosper" (Genesis 39:3). Potiphar, pleased with the young slave he purchased, made him manager over his entire estate.

In his service as captain of the guard for Pharaoh, Potiphar spent a great deal of time away from home. His wife, attracted by a strong, muscular young man, began flirting and making eyes at Joseph. Words of a woman found in Proverbs describe the situation that developed between the slave and his master's wife:

> "I have spread my bed with tapestry,
> Colored coverings of Egyptian linen.
> I have perfumed my bed
> With myrrh, aloes, and cinnamon,
> Come, let us take our fill of love until morning;
> Let us delight ourselves with love.
> For my husband is not at home;
> He has gone on a long journey" (Proverbs 7:16-19).

In Proverbs, the young man takes the bait, gets caught in the trap, and heads for disaster. When Joseph was invited to go to the bedroom, he stood tall with muscles tight. He looked straight into the eyes of his seductress. "How ... can I do this great wickedness, and sin against God?" (Genesis 39:9).

Joseph, far from his father and family, could have reasoned, *It's so lonely here in Egypt. I'm far from home and no one will ever know. Here's a perfect chance to have a little fun.*

Instead Joseph understood what everyone climbing the *ladder* to heaven must learn. It doesn't matter where we are—we are always in the presence of God. We cannot escape His observation. He even knows our thoughts. Adultery or fornication is not only a wicked act, it's sin—sin against ourselves, sin against another, and sin against God.

Day after day, Mrs. Potiphar kept tempting Joseph. "Come on, show me you're a man. Give me a hug. Let me show you how to kiss." The Bible says, "He did not heed her, to lie with her or to be with her" (Genesis 39:10). This is not the end of the story.

One day Joseph entered the mansion to do his work. No one else was around—except Potiphar's wife. Determined to have an affair, the provocative woman suddenly appeared. "We're alone, Joseph. Let's do it!" She grabbed his shirt.

What would this handsome young man do now? "He left his garment in her hand, and fled and ran outside" (Genesis 39:12).

A man of courage, Joseph ran from sin. "Blessed is the man who endures temptation; for when he has been proved, he will receive the crown of life which the Lord has promised to those who love Him" (James 1:12).

Night after night under the stars outside the family tent, Joseph had listened to his father tell about the mystical *ladder* reaching from earth to heaven. Now through faith in Jesus, he remained a virgin, waiting for the day when he would marry and love his wife. He passed the test, becoming an example of *virtue* for all time. Faith leads to *virtue*, and with the help of Jesus, victory over sin and a home in heaven.

Joseph knew there is a price to pay for faithfulness. He didn't have to wait long. Mrs. Potiphar had his shirt. Anxious to revenge a youth who dared to refuse her wishes, she schemed to get even.

"Look at this!" She held up Joseph's shirt when her husband came home. "That scoundrel you put in charge of our property burst into our mansion and tried to rape me. I screamed and he ran, leaving his garment."

Potiphar called for Joseph and hauled him off to the king's prison. Joseph wasted no time worrying about his fate. He didn't question, "Is this what God gives me for doing right? He did everything possible to be cooperative. In a short time, the warden placed him in charge of the prisoners. You know the story. Joseph, a man of *virtue*, ended up as Egypt's Prime Minister. Loving God, Joseph faithfully observed the seventh commandment.

Listed here are seven reasons why God condemns sexual immorality:

1. It destroys the sanctity of marriage and the family. "Marriage is honorable in all, ... but fornicators and adulterers God will judge" (Hebrews 13:4).

2. It's a sin against your own body. "Flee sexual immorality. Every sin that a man does is outside the body, but he who commits sexual immorality sins against his own body" (1 Corinthians 6:18).
3. It causes emotional turmoil. "Abstain from fleshly lusts which war against the soul" (1 Peter 2:11).
4. Sexual immorality destroys our witness to unbelievers. After David sinned with another man's wife, God's prophet warned, "By this deed you have given great occasion to the enemies of the Lord to blaspheme" (2 Samuel 12:14).
5. It leads to ruined lives. "I was on the verge of total ruin" (Proverbs 5:14).
6. It often results in sexual disease and death. "And you mourn at last, when your flesh and your body are consumed" (Proverbs 5:11).
7. It keeps people out of heaven. "Do you know that the unrighteous will not inherit the kingdom of God? Do not be deceived. Neither fornicators, … nor adulterers, nor homosexuals … will inherit the kingdom of God" (1 Corinthians 6:9, 10).

A father spoke to me with tears in his eyes. "The worst mistake I ever made was to buy my son a Porsche." Gary [not his real name] got top grades at a Christian college. The new Porsche, a gift for getting all A's, led to temptation. He began driving to San Francisco on Saturday nights.

Curiosity led him to visit the city's gay bars. Playing with temptation, he became hooked on a homosexual lifestyle. He still managed to graduate from college with honors and landed a good job with an accounting firm.

But less than 10 years out of college, he was forced to ask, "What's wrong with me? Why do I feel so weak?" A medical checkup confirmed his worst fears: HIV positive, AIDS! His health deteriorated rapidly. No longer able to care for himself, loving parents invited him home where his mother gave him constant care. Gary died at 30 from a sexually transmitted disease.

I conducted his memorial service. Only a few days before his death, he assured me his sins were confessed and he was at peace with God. His mother, worn out by the strain of caring for her son, died a few months later.

If you've fallen into sexual sin, whether you're 17 or 71, Jesus says, "Go and sin no more" (John 8:11). David prayed, "Create in me a clean heart, O God" (Psalm 51:10). Paul admonishes, "Let everyone who names the name of Christ depart from iniquity. ... Flee ... youthful lusts. ... Pursue righteousness, faith, love. ... Call on the Lord out of a pure heart" (2 Timothy 2:19, 22). "Walk in the Spirit, and you shall not fulfill the lust of the flesh" (Galatians 5:16).

God gave the seventh commandment for our good and to protect the family. "You shall not commit adultery" (Exodus 20:14). These words prohibit all sex outside of marriage including:

1. Fornication and adultery
2. Divorce and remarriage without Bible grounds
3. Homosexuality and lesbianism
4. Solo sex or masturbation
5. All other sexual sins including incest and sexual abuse

While turning from perversion and sexual sin, we must remember that God created sex to be a blessing for the family, as an expression of a husband's and wife's love for each other. The following Bible verses help us see God's plan for love in the home:

1. "So God created man in His own image; in the image of God He created him; male and female he created them" (Genesis 1:27). He created woman for man, not man for man. "Therefore a man shall ... be joined to his wife and they shall become one flesh" (Genesis 2:24).
2. "Then Isaac brought her into his mother Sarah's tent; and he took Rebekah and she became his wife and *he loved her*" (Genesis 24:67). Jesus says, "Love one

another" (John 15:12). "Rejoice with the wife of your youth. ... Always be enraptured with her love" (Proverbs 5:18, 19). When the husband loves the wife and the wife loves the husband, home becomes a little bit of heaven here on earth.

3. "Let the husband render to his wife the affection due her, and likewise also the wife to her husband. ... Do not deprive one another" (1 Corinthians 7:3, 5).
4. "Wives, submit to your own husbands, as is fitting in the Lord" (Colossians 3:18). Husbands, love your wives, just as Christ also loved the church and gave Himself for it" (Ephesians 5:25).
5. "Above all these things put on love, which is the bond of perfection" (Colossians 4:14). Unselfish love leads to true happiness. God wants husbands and wives to find joy.

Virtue is the result of a pure mind. Jesus said, "Blessed are the pure in heart for they shall see God" (Matthew 5:8). Pure youth, pure men and women will get to the top of the *ladder*. It starts in our mind. "For as he thinks in his heart, so is he" (Proverbs 23:7). "Out of the heart of men, proceed evil thoughts, adulteries, fornications. ... All these evil things come from within and defile a man" (Mark 7:21, 23).

The words of Jesus are straightforward. "Whoever looks at a woman to lust for her has already committed adultery with her in his heart" (Matthew 5:28).

In order to think pure thoughts, we must shun all evil sounds and sights. Job says, "I have made a covenant with my eyes; why then should I look upon a young woman?" (Job 31:1). We may have to turn off the TV, avoid renting Hollywood videos and going to movies, refuse to view pornography, get rid of sensual publications—anything that would lead us to think evil.

Christians heading for heaven will only visit sites on the Internet that reflect the highest values. We will avoid all impure speech. "But fornication and all uncleanness or covetousness, let it not be named among you, as is fitting for saints; neither filthiness, nor foolish talking, nor coarse jesting, which are not fitting, but rather giving thanks" (Ephesians 5:3, 4).

Sins of sex are one of the signs of the last days. Impurity and immorality leap out at us on every side. Victory over sin means fixing our eyes on Jesus alone and with His help, doing His will.

In a world saturated with sex, it's too easy to want to do everything other people do. Fooling around. Touching, handling, fondling. Making out, going all the way. This is not God's plan for people preparing to live with Him in heaven.

A group of young people were discussing proper conduct with the opposite sex. A girl from Brazil said this: "We should not do anything with the opposite sex that affects us below the belt." Good advice! Once the fire gets burning, it's hard to put it out. God's plan is to wait until you're married.

Condoms are promoted around the world today. They call it *safe sex*. There is no such thing as *safe sin*. But you ask, "Didn't God forgive David?"

Yes, God forgave David, and He can forgive you. But remember, David suffered the consequences of his sin all the rest of His life.

My wife, Evelyn, and I lived in an apartment near a university campus. About 10:00 o'clock one evening, we heard loud talking on the street outside. A university girl screamed at her boy friend. "Can't you understand? I've already had several abortions. It's not worth it just to have a little fun!"

God's call to a life of *virtue* not only prepares us for heaven—it helps us right now to:

1. Safeguard the purity of family relations
2. Avert emotional conflicts
3. Avoid teenage pregnancy and abortion
4. Enjoy freedom from sexually transmitted diseases
5. Prepare for a happy marriage that will be blessed by God

In our wicked world, too much lovemaking goes on before marriage and often too little after. Spouses hate each other and end up in divorce. Our Creator knows exactly what He is doing by asking us to remain virgins until marriage. Jesus invites us to live lives of *virtue* and trust in Him for victory. He wants us to get to the top of the *ladder*. He wants us to enjoy life now and spend eternity in heaven with Him.

"Finally, … whatever things are pure, whatever things are lovely, whatever things are of good report, if there is any *virtue* … meditate on these things" (Philippians 4:8). Cling to Jesus and take the step of *virtue*. His Word promises, "My God shall supply all your need according to His riches in glory by Christ Jesus" (Philippians 4:19).

I will live a life of VIRTUE,
Live in purity.

Points to Remember

1. Jesus has a place reserved in heaven for those who live pure lives.
2. The Savior asks us to live lives of *virtue.*
3. *Virtue* is the result of escaping the corruption that is in the world through lust.
4. Sexual sins are a sign of the last days.
5. Jesus is able to keep us from falling into sin.
6. All sex outside of marriage between a man and woman is sin.
7. The seventh commandment guards the purity of the family.
8. Jesus can forgive sin and give us strength to live pure lives.
9. Victory over sin comes by fixing our eyes on Jesus, and with His help, doing His will.

Climb Higher

God's Invitation to Purity
"The corruption of the world is seeking to steal our senses. ... To draw us away from all this is the precious *ladder.* ... The invitation comes, ... Come up higher ... Higher and still higher we ascend. ... Higher, holier ambitions take possession of the soul. The guilt of the past life is left behind. ... We lay hold on Christ, climbing up by Christ, resolving to return, broken, contrite, subdued, to the Father above the *ladder*" (*Manuscript Releases,* 19:346).

"Faith, *virtue,* ... [are rounds] of the *ladder.* We are saved by climbing round after round, mounting step after step, to the height of Christ's ideal for us" (Translated from *Los Hechos de los Apostoles,* 422. Compare with *The Acts of the Apostles,* 530).

The Ladder

"**Jesus the precious Saviour** ... is the *ladder* uniting the celestial world with the terrestrial. His divinity lays hold of the throne of God. His humanity touches the earth. His human arm encircles the entire human race" (*That I May Know Him*, 328).

"**In his childhood, Joseph had been taught the love and fear of God.** Often in his father's tent, under the Syrian stars, he had been told the story ... of the *ladder* from heaven to earth" (*Education*, 52).

"**Angels of God**, that ascend and descend the *ladder* which Jacob saw in vision, will help every soul who will, to climb even to the highest heaven" (*Patriarchs and Prophets*, 568).

The Step of Virtue

"If there is any *virtue* . . . meditate on these things" (Philippians 4:8).

"**The things that defile the soul** must be banished from the mind and life. When temptations are presented, they must be resisted in the strength of Christ. The *virtue* of the spotless Lamb of God must be woven into the character till the soul can stand in its integrity. ... Joseph is an example of how the youth may stand unspotted, amid the evil of the world, and add to their faith, *virtue*" (*My Life Today*, 96).

"**Let the young ever remember** that wherever they are, and whatever they do, they are in the presence of God. No part of our conduct escapes observation" (*Patriarchs and Prophets*, 217).

"**The way of the believer** is marked out by God above the *ladder*. All his endeavors will be in vain if he has not *virtue* of character" (*Our High Calling*, 68).

God's Plan for Marriage

"It is not good that man should be alone; I will make him a helper comparable to him. ... Man shall leave his father and mother and be joined to his wife" (Genesis 2:18, 24).

"They are no longer two but one flesh. Therefore what God has joined together, let not man separate" (Matthew 19:6).

"But I say to you that whoever divorces his wife for any reason except sexual immorality causes her to commit adultery; and whoever marries a woman who is divorced commits adultery" (Matthew 5:32).

"Let none deal treacherously with the wife of his youth. For the Lord God of Israel says that He hates divorce" (Malachi 2:15, 16).

Love in Marriage

"Wives, submit to your own husbands, as is fitting in the Lord. Husbands love your wives and do not be bitter toward them" (Colossians 3:18, 19).

"**Love is a precious gift**, which we receive from Jesus" (*Messages to Young People*, 425).

"**Love cannot long exist without expression**. Let not the heart of one connected with you starve for the want of kindness and sympathy. ... Though difficulties, perplexities, and discouragements may arise, let neither husband nor wife harbor the thought that their union is a mistake or a disappointment. Determine to be all that it is possible to be to each other. Continue the early attentions. In every way encourage each other in fighting the battles of life. Study to advance the happiness of each other. Let there be mutual love, mutual forbearance. Then marriage, instead of being the end of love, will be as it were the very beginning of love. The warmth of true friendship, the love that binds heart to heart, is a foretaste of the joys of heaven" (*The Ministry of Healing*, 360).

"**Let each give love** rather than exact it" (*The Ministry of Healing*, 361).

The Privileges of Marriage

"Let the husband render to his wife the affection due her, and likewise also the wife to her husband. The wife does not have authority over her own body, but the husband does. And likewise the husband does not have authority over his own body, but the wife does. Do not deprive one another except with consent for a time, that you may give yourselves to fasting and prayer; and come together again so that Satan does not tempt you because of your lack of self-control" (1 Corinthians 7:3-5).

"**The family tie** is the closest, the most tender and sacred, of any on earth. It was designed to be a blessing to mankind" (*The Ministry of Healing*, 356).

Preparing for Marriage

"Do not be unequally yoked together with unbelievers" (2 Corinthians 6:14).

"**Let those who are contemplating marriage** weigh every sentiment and watch every development of character in the one with whom they think to unite their life destiny. Let every step toward a marriage alliance be characterized by modesty, simplicity, sincerity, and an earnest purpose to please and honor God" (*Messages to Young People*, 435).

"**Let the questions be raised**, Will this union help me heavenward? Will it increase my love for God? . . . Will it enlarge my sphere of usefulness in this life? If these reflections present no drawback, then in the fear of God move forward" (*Messages to Young People*, 449).

"**True love is a high and holy principle**. . . . It is by faithfulness to duty in the parental home that the youth are to prepare themselves for homes of their own. . . . Marriage instead of being the end of love, will be only its beginning" (*Messages to Young People*, 466).

Blessings of a Spouse

"A prudent wife is from the Lord" (Proverbs 10:14).

"He who finds a wife finds a good thing, and obtains favor from the Lord" (Proverbs 18:22).

"**Men and women** can reach God's ideal for them if they will take Christ as their helper. . . . His providence can unite hearts in bonds that are of heavenly origin" (*The Adventist Home*, 112).

Chapter 4
The Greatest Invention

Jesus proclaims, *"I am the WAY, the truth and the life.*
No one comes to the Father except through me."
—John 14:6

We are saved by climbing with Jesus.
Steps up the *ladder* include faith, virtue, and SCIENCE.

*L*ike most people, I don't remember my first ride in an automobile. After my birth at Cottage Hospital in Santa Barbara, California, Dad loaded Mother and me into his black Model T Ford. He cranked the engine, climbed in, and we were off to my grandfather Davis's farm at Casitas Pass some 30 miles away. Having never heard of seat belts or child seats, Mother held me tight all the way.

When I turned six, Dad traded the Model T in on a second hand De Soto. I jumped up and down when he drove into our yard. Mom hugged Dad and started crying. "Mama, why are you crying?" I asked. "You should be glad we have a new car!"

Mother took my hand. "When you get a little older, you will understand. I know this is a better car, but the old Model T has so many memories." Memories? What I remember about the old Model T is my dad working on it every Sunday, almost all day, to keep it running.

Thirty-five years later, while serving as missionaries in Peru, we imported a Ford station wagon from Germany. I remembered how the old Model T struggled to get up to 35 miles an hour. The German Ford's tiny four-cylinder engine, however, proved to be a remarkable piece of scientific engineering. Driving home from a trip on the coast, I decided to see how fast the German Ford could go. I had no traffic and a straight road for miles. I pushed the accelerator to the floor and watched the speedometer climb to 70 miles per hour, the 80, 90, 100, 105. I held my breath. When it hit 110, I took my foot off the gas. As the little Ford slowed, I couldn't help but think, *It's amazing how quickly science has increased from my parents' Model T to this!*

As a boy, my parents had no radio. One day my dad came home with a crystal set. He spent the evening turning the knobs. It made so much noise, he returned it the next day and got his money back. After a few months, he bought a Sears Silvertone shortwave radio that brought in programs from around the world! Then many years ago, while serving in Peru, I traveled deep in the Amazon Jungle. We stopped at a small village. An Indian, his face painted red, came running out of the forest. He said, "Robert Kennedy has just been shot." He carried a little Japanese transistor radio. The *science* of communication has leaped forward at unbelievable speed during my lifetime. Crystal sets, tubes, transistors, television, satellite transmission, and now the Internet and the World Wide Web. Our daughters serve as missionaries on opposite sides the world, but we keep instantly in touch with e-mails!

While still in the eighth grade, I spent my life savings to buy a secondhand Remington Rand portable typewriter. As a young minister, I spent three months' salary to buy an office typewriter. Today for less than one months' salary, I can buy a high-end desktop computer. I'm sitting in front of one right now. It's loaded with word processing, 16 different Bibles, Ellen G. White software, a Bible Commentary, the *Encyclopedia Britannica* that includes *Webster's Collegiate Dictionary*, PageMaker, PhotoShop, Netscape and more. I'm constantly amazed at how *science* jumps ahead every day.

I was only a toddler when Charles Lindbergh made headlines by flying solo across the Atlantic. On our first trip to South America as missionaries, we flew on an old DC-4. It took three days to fly from San Francisco to Lima. Later, on a flight from Lima to Santiago, the captain on our Boeing 707 announced, "We are flying 1,000 kilometers an hour," that's 600 miles every 60 minutes. I'd never flown that fast before. *Compared to this*, I thought, *my German Ford at 110 miles an hour barely crawls.*

A few months later, I led a delegation from Peru, Bolivia, and Ecuador to attend a World Youth Congress in Switzerland. We changed planes in Frankfurt. While boarding our last flight, an announcement came over the intercom that I did not understand. German-speaking passengers applauded. Then the same voice announced in English, "Americans have just landed on the moon, and we are very happy." I applauded.

During their flight, the astronauts accelerated to 24,245 miles per hour—more than 40 times faster than the Boeing 707 jet traveled on its flight to Santiago. Jumbo jets flying around the world today just lumber along in comparison to the speed of the moon flight.

In the hotel lobby that night, we crowded around a television set to see Neil Armstrong climb out of the Lunar Module and take his first step on the moon. He exclaimed, "That's one small step for a man, one giant leap for mankind." That's what this book is about. Taking steps. Not steps on the powdery surface of the moon, but climbing the *ladder* of progress step by step all the way to heaven. The greatest step forward will be when we step off the *ladder* into God's eternal kingdom.

Whether you're a teenager or a senior citizen, you know that *science* has increased rapidly in your lifetime. God spoke 2,500 years ago saying, "Daniel, shut up the words, and seal the book until the time of the end; many shall run to and fro, and knowledge shall increase" (Daniel 12:4). My Spanish Bible says, "*Science* shall be multiplied." We've seen more progress in the acceleration of *science* during the last 50 years than in the previous 5,000.

Is Daniel talking about an increased understanding of Bible prophecy since the time of the end began in 1798 or the amazing developments in travel, information, and communications?

Or perhaps both? One thing is for sure: Daniel is a special book for the time of the end, and the focus is on Christ and the cross. Referring to the book of Daniel, Jesus says, "Whoever reads, let him understand" (Matthew 24:15).

Daniel, Jesus, and John help us understand:

1. The investigative or pre-advent judgment began in 1844.
2. Jesus is our judge.
3. Jesus is our intercessor.
4. Jesus, the Lamb of God, died on the cross to save us from sin.
5. We need to be ready, "for the Son of Man is coming at an hour when you do not expect Him" (Matthew 24:44).

Fabulous advances in *science* make it possible to quickly take the good news of Jesus and the *science* of the cross around the globe. The Savior said, "This gospel of the kingdom will be preached in all the world as a witness to all the nations, and then the end will come" (Matthew 24:14). The last prayer in the Bible is one I pray every day. "Even so, come, Lord Jesus" (Revelation 22:20). In this same verse, Jesus promises, "I am coming quickly."

My old camera is not the point-and-shoot kind. To get a sharp picture, it must be focused carefully. Likewise, we must focus carefully on Jesus to experience righteousness by faith. We'll never get to heaven unless we trust in Him. We've looked at faith and virtue. You may be surprised to learn that the next step on the *ladder* to heaven is *science.*

Science and technical knowledge led to the creation of automobiles, airplanes, radio, TV, video, computers, the Internet, satellite communication, and space travel. These inventions and thousands more are only possible because of the greatest invention of all. It happened on the sixth day of creation. "So God created man in His own image" (Genesis 1:27).

Inside the heads of men and women, Jesus placed some 10 billion brain cells. Human beings can love or hate, do right or wrong—choose. They can invent. Scripture says "God …

made man upright; but they have sought out many inventions" (Ecclesiastes 7:29, KJV). Sadly, humans "provoked Him to anger with their inventions" (Psalm 106:29, KJV). God looked down and saw "the wickedness of man ... in the earth, and that every imagination of the thoughts of his heart *was* only evil continually" (Genesis 6:5, KJV). "Thus were they defiled with their own works" (Psalm 106:39).

Inventions by the world's top scientists put men on the moon. Only Jesus can put you and me in heaven. The knowledge I need more than anything else is the *science of the cross.*

It happened on a lonely hill outside Jerusalem. Golgotha. Calvary—"the place of the skull." Men drove cruel nails through the hands and feet of the Creator of the universe. Blood flowed as the Son of God hung on a cross. Pain beyond comprehension penetrated every nerve and fiber of His body. More terrible than the crown of thorns or the nails, agony for the sins of the world, my sins and your sins, weighed on His mind. He suffered for you and for me.

Isaiah describes it well. "He is despised and rejected by men. ... He has born our griefs and carried our sorrows. ... He was wounded for our transgressions. He was bruised for our iniquities. ... All we like sheep have gone astray; we have turned, every one, to his own way; and the Lord has laid on Him the iniquity of us all" (Isaiah 53:3, 5, 6).

Why did Jesus die on the cross? It's because "all have sinned" and "the wages of sin is death "(Romans 3:23, 6:23). "Death spread to all men because all sinned" (Romans 5:12). The mission of our Savior is to "save His people from their sins" (Matthew 1:21). He wants to save you. He wants to save me.

In chapter one, I told you that I rebelled against my parents—I called my mother a slave driver, I ran away from home. I broke the commandment that says, "Honor your father and your mother" (Exodus 20:12). And if that's not enough, God's Word declares, "For whoever shall keep the whole law, and yet stumble in one *point,* he is guilty of all" (James 2:10). Whether we take God's name in vain, tell a lie, commit adultery, or even kill someone, the penalty is the same—death. And eternal death at that!

Facing the death penalty, I want to be good, but even my best is only "filthy rags." I can't change if I wanted. "For what I will to do, that I do not ... but what I hate, that I do. ... O wretched man that I am! Who shall deliver me from this body of death?" (Romans 7:15, 24).

Is there an answer to my predicament? "I thank God there is a way out through Jesus Christ our Lord" (Romans 7:25, Phillips). The solution to my problem is found in the *science* of the cross. Jesus died to rescue me from sin. He offers life, not death.

Hungry after an early breakfast and hours of driving to reach San Francisco, Bob and I, on assignment to help with Bay-area evangelism, looked for a place to park. A car ahead pulled out. Large green letters on a sign posted on the street said, "One Hour Parking." I parallel parked my new Pontiac with care.

We ate at Clinton's Cafeteria overlooking Market Street. "Bob," I said as we were finishing strawberry shortcake for desert. "I think the hour on our parking meter is almost up." We paid our bill and hurried back to Golden Gate Street to pick up the car.

Reaching the exact spot where we'd parked, I stopped in amazement. "Bob, there's no car! What's going on?" I shouted, "This is where we parked the car. Here's the sign that says, 'One Hour Parking.' Somebody stole my new car!"

"I know this is the right street," Bob said. We looked up and down, but no black Pontiac. A sinking feeling made me wish I'd gone without dinner. In desperation, I phoned the San Francisco police department. "My car's been stolen!" I said.

"Where did you park?" the policeman asked. "I parked on Golden Gate Street."

"What time did you park your car?"

"Oh, it was about 15 minutes before 12:00."

"When did you find it missing?"

"About 21 minutes to 1:00."

"Sir," the police officer continued: "Don't you know that no parking is allowed on Golden Gate Street after 12 noon? Your car probably got towed away by the police. Did you say it's a black Pontiac? Give me the license number and I'll check."

I held the phone. *No parking after 12:00! How was I supposed to know?*

The policeman came back on the line. "Your car is in the police parking lot at the corner of Ellis and Taylor. You will have to go there to get it."

Greatly relieved, I told Bob, "They've got my car. We can go pick it up."

Back on the street we looked at the sign. Large green letters jumped out at me, "One Hour Parking." But now I read the small red letters below the large green ones. "No Parking after 12:00 noon."

I broke the law. They towed my car. Arriving at the police parking lot, I announced, "I've come to pick up my car." The officer looked at me. "You can have your car, but first you will have to pay a $140 fine."

"One-hundred forty dollars! I don't have $140."

"OK," the officer said. "Come back when you have the money. We will charge you storage for every day your car stays here."

Back out on the street, I spoke with Bob. "Bringing a brand-new car to San Francisco was not a very smart idea. I failed to read the fine print on the parking sign, and now I'm without a car. I don't have money to pay the fine."

He reached for his billfold. "I brought some extra cash. I'll lend you the money."

"I hate to take your money, but you are sure getting me out of a mess. I'll pay you back when I get my next check." I walked back into the police parking lot, paid the fine, picked up the car, and we drove away to meet with members of our evangelistic team.

I had a lot to think about. *Satan hijacked planet earth. We're all held hostage in the devil's parking lot of sin. My friend loaned me money, but Jesus has done much more. Our sins put us on death row. He gave His blood to save us from the penalty of death.*

By His death on the cross, "He has delivered us from the power of darkness and translated us into the kingdom of the Son of His love, in whom we have the forgiveness of sins. ... For by Him all things were created that are in heaven and that are on earth. ... For it pleased the Father that in Him all the fullness should dwell, and by Him to reconcile all things to Himself, by Him, whether things on earth or things in heaven, having made peace through the blood of His cross. ... He has reconciled in the body of His flesh through death, to present you holy, and blameless, and irreproachable in His sight—if indeed you continue in the faith" (Colossians 1:13, 14, 16, 19-22).

While serving in Bangkok, Thailand, I learned about a Chinese couple who immigrated to New York City. Hard work brought them success. They moved into a fine apartment with their children. Suddenly without warning, tragedy struck. Both husband and wife died, leaving their two sons orphaned. The older boy encouraged his younger brother. "I love you," he said. "I will drop out of school and work so you can get your education." The younger brother studied hard and got excellent grades. But then things began to change. Grades dropped. Drugs, alcohol, gambling—he joined a street gang and became involved in crime.

This young man spent more and more time in a dingy gambling den hoping to win money to pay for his vices. He did well and often walked away with pockets filled with cash. Then one evening, he played a game and lost everything.

Suddenly he realized, *This other guy didn't win. He cheated! It was no win at all.* The two men got into a fight. The immigrant's son reached for a knife. "You can't cheat me like this!" He screamed. He stabbed his gambling companion in the chest. Once. Twice. Three times. The man who cheated fell to the floor. The young man with the knife looked down. The man was dead.

The youth fled back to the apartment where he lived with his brother. He searched the place and took all his brother's money. He pulled off his dirty, torn, blood stained clothes, rolled them up and shoved them to the back of the closet. He put on clean clothes, raced to the railroad station, bought a ticket and boarded a train heading out of New York City.

There were two things the young murderer did not know: First, the cleaning lady, an old woman, saw him kill the other man. Second, his brother had been in the apartment and saw the horror and fear on his face when he came in.

The elder brother thought for a moment. *My brother is in trouble. I wonder what he's done now?* He went to the bedroom and took off his clothes. Reaching deep into the back of the closet, he pulled out his brother's bloodstained clothes and put them on. He walked back to the living room, sat down, and waited.

There was a knock at the door. The police arrested him and hauled him off to jail. He looked like his brother. At the trial the cleaning woman even identified him as the killer, and he was sentenced to be executed.

Ten years later, the murderer returned to New York City and searched for his older brother. He went to the apartment. No one there had even heard of his brother. Finally, in desperation, he went to the police station. He gave the officer his brother's name.

"I remember him well," he said. "I arrested him."

"Why did you arrest him? He was the best brother a fellow could have. After our parents died, he worked so I could go to school. What happened after the arrest?"

"We put him in jail," the officer replied.

"Then what?" The younger brother wanted to know.

"He was tried for murder and found guilty."

"What happened then?"

"He was executed."

The murderer broke down and wept. "You executed the wrong man! I'm the murderer!" He fully expected to be tried for his crime and die.

The officer explained: "We only execute one man for a crime. Your bother paid your penalty. You're a free man."

The older brother did what the Savior does for us. Jesus offers to take our filthy rags and give us His robe of righteousness. He died so we can live. "The Lord ... laid on Him the iniquity of us all" (Isaiah 53:6).

The One who made me also died on the cross to save me, and He's coming back to take me home. In His greatest invention, the crowning act of creation, Jesus made a mind that can choose between right and wrong. We can love and obey or we can rebel and go our own way. Instead of programming us like a computer, He invites us in love, "come, take up the cross, and follow Me" (Mark 10:21).

The *science* of the cross is one giant leap toward heaven. It's a step we must take with Jesus. We are challenged: "Let this mind be in you which was also in Christ Jesus. ... He humbled Himself and became obedient to *the point of* death, even the death of the cross" (Philippians 2:5, 8).

By climbing the *ladder* we are "looking unto Jesus, ... who for the joy that was set before Him endured the cross" (*Hebrews 12:2*). His joy is saving sinners and helping us reach heaven. "Jesus ... loved us and washed us from our sins in His own blood" (Revelation 1:5). Why? He wants us to be among those who "washed their robes and made them white in the blood of the Lamb" (Revelation 7:14). This is the *science* of the cross, a mystery we will study for eternity.

I will search God's Word for knowledge,
The SCIENCE of the cross.
Points to Remember

1. Jesus created us.
2. We were made in the image of God—upright and without sin.
3. He gave us rules to live by.
4. We broke the rules.
5. All have sinned and face the death penalty.
6. We are helpless and can not save ourselves.
7. Jesus paid the penalty for our sins on the cross.
8. He shed His blood to save us.
9. The blood of Jesus cleanses us from sin
10. The science of the cross will be our study for eternity.

Climb Higher

God Offers His Science

"Climb higher and still higher" (*Counsels to Teachers*, 269).

"Faith, virtue, *science* ... [are rounds] of the *ladder*. We are saved by climbing round after round, mounting step after step, to the height of Christ's ideal for us" (Translated from *Los Hechos de los Apostoles*, 422. Compare with *The Acts of the Apostles*, 530).

"**Every sinner may come to Christ**. 'Not by works of righteousness which we have done, but according to His mercy He saved us.' Titus 3:5. When Satan tells you that you are a sinner, and cannot hope to receive blessing from God, tell him that Christ came into the world to save sinners. We have nothing to recommend us to God; but the plea that we may urge now and ever is our utterly helpless condition that makes His redeeming power a necessity. Renouncing all self-dependence, we may look to the cross of Calvary and say,—'In my hand no price I bring; Simply to Thy cross I cling" (*The Desire of Ages*, 317).

The Ladder

"**The steps to heaven must be taken one at a time**, and every advance step gives strength for the next" (*Counsels to Parents, Teachers and Students*, 100).

"**The whole *science* of salvation** is contained in accepting Christ as a personal, sin-pardoning Saviour" (*Manuscript Releases*, 3:339).

"**Justice** demands that sin be not merely pardoned, but the death penalty must be executed. God, in the gift of His only-begotten Son, met both these requirements. By dying in man's stead, Christ exhausted the penalty and provided a pardon" (*God's Amazing Grace*, 139).

"**Without the cross, man could have no union with the Father.** On it depends our every hope. From it shines the light of the Saviour's love, and when at the foot of the cross the sinner looks up to the One who died to save him, he may rejoice with fullness of joy, for his sins are pardoned. Kneeling in faith at the cross, he has reached the highest place to which man can attain" (*The Acts of the Apostles*, 209, 210).

The Science of the Cross

"**The cross of Christ will be the *science*** and the song of the redeemed through all eternity. … Never will it be forgotten that He whose power created and upheld the unnumbered worlds through the vast realms of space … humbled Himself to uplift fallen man; that He bore the guilt and shame of sin … till the woes of a lost world broke His heart and crushed out His life on Calvary's cross. … 'Worthy, worthy is the Lamb that was slain, and hath redeemed us to God by His own most precious blood!'" (*The Great Controversy*, 651, 652).

"**Let the cross of Christ be made the *science* of all education.** … Let it be brought into the daily experience in practical life. So will the Saviour become to the youth a daily companion and friend" (*The Ministry of Healing*, 460).

"**The cross of Calvary** … is true philosophy, pure and undefiled religion. It is eternal life to all who believe" (*Sons and Daughters of God*, 231).

"**Christ's death proves God's great love for man**. It is our pledge of salvation. To remove the cross from the Christian would be like blotting the sun from the sky" (*The Acts of the Apostles*, 209).

The Mystery of the Cross

"The message of the cross is foolishness to those who are perishing, but to us who are being saved it is the power of God" (1 Corinthians 1:18).

"**The mystery of the cross explains all other mysteries.** In the light that streams from Calvary the attributes of God which had filled us with fear and awe appear beautiful and attractive. Mercy, tenderness, and parental love are seen to blend with holiness, justice, and power" (*The Great Controversy*, 652).

"**Justification by faith** is to many a mystery. A sinner is justified by God when he repents of his sins. He sees Jesus upon the cross of Calvary. . . . He looks to the atoning Sacrifice as his only hope" (*Our High Calling, 52*).

"**As we behold the Lamb of God upon the cross** of Calvary, the mystery of redemption begins to unfold to our minds and the goodness of God leads us to repentance. In dying for sinners, Christ manifested a love that is incomprehensible." (*Steps to Christ*, 26, 27).

Take Up Your Cross

"Whoever desires to come after Me, let him deny himself, and take up his cross, and follow Me" (Mark 8:34).

"**We must deny self, take up the cross,** and follow Jesus. Not one of us can reach heaven, save by the narrow, cross-bearing way" (*Lift Him Up*, 245).

"**Lift the cross,** and it will lift you. It will be to you a pledge of eternal life" (*Pacific Union Recorder*, March 2, 1905).

"**The light shining from the cross reveals the love of God**. His love is drawing us to Himself. If we do not resist this drawing, we shall be led to the foot of the cross in repentance for the sins that have crucified the Saviour. Then the Spirit of God through faith produces a new life in the soul. The thoughts and desires are brought into obedience to the will of Christ. The heart, the mind, are created anew in the image of Him who works in us to subdue all things to Himself. Then the law of God is written in the mind and heart, and we can say with Christ, 'I delight to do Thy will, O my God.' Ps. 40:8" (*The Desire of Ages*, 175).

Chapter 5
Eight Ways
to Stay Alive

Jesus proclaims, "I am the WAY, the truth and the life.
No one comes to the Father except through me."
—**John 14:6**

We are saved by climbing with Jesus.
Steps up the *ladder* include faith, science,
and TEMPERANCE.

My brother, Don, and I took inner tubes and plunged into the Pacific Ocean north of Morro Rock on the California Coast. We struggled to swim past pounding breakers. Finally, we were far enough from shore to relax and enjoy the thrill of riding over giant waves.

Don stayed in the water clinging to his inner tube. *I want to see more,* I thought and pulled myself out of the water and up on top of the tube. *This is great!* Each new swell lifted me high for a great view. Sitting on the inner tube and using my hands for paddles, I moved around just like riding in a small boat.

"You ought to try this," I called to Don.

"No way, " he responded. "It's a lot warmer in this cold water than out there in the wind."

Boy, I do feel cold! I looked at my arms. Goose bumps! *And I'm shivering all over.* I looked back toward the shoreline. *What a fantastic view,* I thought. Suddenly I realized, *This stiff cold breeze is blowing us out to sea.*

"I'm going back!" I shouted to my brother.

"I'm coming too," he said. "We'd better try to stay together."

Slipping back into the water, I tried to swim and drag the inner tube toward shore. *What's wrong?* I asked myself. *My energy's gone. I feel awful.* I wrestled to swim against the wind. Each stroke brought little headway as the outgoing tide sucked me back toward the sea. My brother, far ahead now, managed to ride a big wave almost all the way to shore. *At least he's safe,* I thought. Cold and weak, I finally reached the heavy surf.

Tons of water poured over me. Waves crashed on my head. I lost the inner tube. *I'm not going to make it. I might as well give up.* Finally my toes touched sand and I started walking to shore. Coming out of the water I realized, *I can hardly stand up. I'll fall.* Don looked at me at laughed. "You look like an old man." *If he only knew,* I thought. *I feel like I'm going to die.*

My parents had been watching and drove their car out on the beach. *Something's wrong with me,* I realized. *I want to live,* I decided and made one desperate attempt to reach the car. My mother opened the front door. I threw myself across the front seat. Everything went black.

The next thing I knew, I was wrapped in a blanket, the car engine was running, the heater was on, and my mother and dad were massaging my arms and legs, trying to get me warm.

My body temperature dropped dangerously low while I rode the waves sitting in the cold breeze on top of an inner tube. You can be sure I'll never forget that Fourth of July at the beach. I could have died from hypothermia. Seeing my parents on the shore, I determined to live. They saved my life.

You and I are headed for heaven. God, the Father, waits for us. He provided a *ladder*, Jesus. We are weak and insecure. The devil tries to convince us we can never make it. Then one look at the loving face of Jesus and we determine to climb with Him. We take one step at a time. Faith, virtue, science, and *temperance.*

Temperance! It's the fourth step—half way up the *ladder.* As long as we cling to Jesus and climb with Him, we can be sure of heaven.

Fearing I'd never make it while struggling to reach shore that day, I suddenly discovered that life is very attractive. Jesus says, "I am come that they may have life, and that they may have it more abundantly" (John 10:10). The Savior who died on the cross to save us not only wants us to have eternal life, He wants us to enjoy abundant living now.

True faith in Jesus includes *temperance*. Scripture records that "Felix ... sent for Paul, and heard him concerning the faith in Christ. ... [Paul] reasoned of righteousness, *temperance*, and judgment to come" (Acts 24:24, 25, KJV). *Temperance* and righteousness by faith go together.

"The fruit of the Spirit is ... *temperance*" among other things (Galatians 5:22, 23, KJV). The popular understanding of *temperance* today is moderation. True Christian *temperance* is complete self-control with total abstinence from all that is harmful and moderation in what is beneficial. We choose to honor Jesus by taking the best possible care of our body temple.

Eight steps up the *ladder* with Jesus take us to the kingdom. And interestingly searching Scripture we find eight important ways to stay alive, have better health and live the abundant life. In order to stay alive we must breathe, sun, abstain, rest, exercise, eat, water and trust. You've noticed these are all action verbs. Let's look at each one.

1. Breathe

Holding my breath long enough to swim the length of a pool always proved a challenge. And snorkeling off the coast of Bermuda, though it provided opportunity to see parts of the Creator's handiwork, I didn't know existed, proved to have one major problem: Every time I dove down to get closer to exotic fish, I could never hold my breath as long as I wanted.

Stop breathing very long, and you pass out. Next comes brain damage. And if you stop breathing for too long, you're dead. The Bible says, "And the Lord God formed man of the dust of the ground, and breathed into his nostrils the breath of life; and man became a living being" (Genesis 2:7).

The oxygen brought into our body by the air we breathe provides life. If you've ever watched someone die, you know the opposite takes place at death. "When his breath departs he returns to his earth" (Psalm 146:4, RSV).

An Old Testament prophet presents a picture of what takes place in the resurrection. "Thus says the Lord God to these bones: 'Surely I will cause breath to enter into you, and you shall live" (Ezekiel 37:5).

Without a constant supply of oxygen, our life ceases to exist. The average adult takes about 16 breaths a minute— about six liters of air. With activity this may be increased to 50 liters.

For optimum health, *breathe* pure unpolluted air. The best quality air is found far away from great centers of population. The air in Bangkok, where my wife and I lived for two years, was so bad that police often wore gas masks. Now we live near 3,000 feet elevation in the foothills of the Sierra Nevada Mountains. The air is not perfect, but it's better than in any large city.

Lung capacity can be improved by breathing deeply. Deep breathing and using abdominal muscles correctly even improves voice quality. It helps avoid tuberculosis and other pulmonary diseases. It improves the function of the brain.

Breathing tobacco smoke, or any other smoke, poses a serious threat to health. Tobacco contains poisons that definitely shorten life. It can cause lung cancer, heart disease, and many other ailments.

Are you addicted? Remember that with Jesus, you can break the habit. The best plan is never to smoke the first cigarette or cigar (or use tobacco in any other form). Instead of wasting money destroying your health, spend that money on worthwhile things.

I thank God for giving me the courage never to put a cigarette in my mouth. I'm grateful that smoking is no longer allowed on most airlines. My lungs belong to Jesus, and I want to give them the best possible care.

2. Sun

Figure out a way to travel 93 million miles into space, and you'll reach an amazing ball of fire. But please don't try it—with a surface temperature around 11,000 degrees Fahrenheit, the sun will burn you up long before you get there.

What would happen if the light from the sun suddenly went out? The water floating in the atmosphere would freeze and fall in deluges of blinding snow. Every river, every lake, every sea would become solid ice. With temperatures falling hundreds of degrees below the freezing point, no life, plant or animal, could exist even for one hour!

Scripture declares, "God is light and in Him is no darkness at all" (1 John 1:5). Jesus placed the sun in the heavens for our benefit. To stay alive, we must sun. Sun? That's right. We need to spend some time sunning outdoors every day. The Creator wants us to enjoy the warm sunlight made by Him for our good.

Solomon wrote, "There is profit to them that see the sun" (Ecclesiastes 7:11, KJV). Jesus said, "He makes His sun rise on the evil and on the good" (Matthew 5:45). Sunlight is filled with blessings, but just a word of caution. Too much sun may cause painful sunburn. Too much sunning may lead to skin cancer. An overdose of what is good may prove harmful.

Students spend a great deal of time in classrooms. Most workers stay inside offices. Too many use most of their leisure time indoors in front of a TV. A real danger for most is not getting enough sun.

Pull back the drapes and flood your home with sunshine. Don't worry if the carpets and furniture fade. Sunlight can actually sanitize your home and kill germs. A healthy room is a sunny room. When you build a house, put in as many windows as possible.

"Remember now your Creator in the days of your youth … while the sun and the light, the moon and the stars, are not darkened" (Ecclesiastes 12:1, 2). "God made two great lights: the greater light to rule the day, and the lesser light to rule the night" (Genesis 1:16).

The ultraviolet rays in sunlight produce vitamin D in humans. This is important in the process of absorbing calcium to form healthy bones. Without sunlight, plants die and so will you. Plan to stay alive. Take time for fun in the sun.

3. Abstain

A teenager invited to eat at a king's table proved to be an ideal role model for anyone who wants to live a life of *temperance*. "Daniel purposed in his heart that he would not defile himself with the portion of the king's delicacies, nor with the wine which he drank" (Daniel 1:8).

Why would a young man refuse to drink alcoholic beverages? Daniel grew up in a home where his parents loved God and gave him a godly education. Here's a Bible verse he would have been familiar with: "Wine is a mocker, strong drink is a brawler, and whoever is led astray by it is not wise" (Proverbs 20:1).

Daniel would also agree with the words of Paul written some 500 years after he refused to drink wine with Nebuchadnezzar: "Do you not know that the unrighteous will not inherit the kingdom of God? … Drunkards … will [not] inherit the kingdom of God" (1 Corinthians 6:9, 10). One out of nine who take the first drink will become alcoholics. Youth who want to reach the top of the *ladder* will not take the risk.

God's commandment states clearly: "You shall not kill" (Exodus 20:13, RSV). Alcohol causes accidents and death. The use of any harmful substance shortens life by slowly destroying our bodies. Because we love God, we will not want to kill ourselves—even slowly. Those who climb the *ladder* with Jesus will learn to say, "No!"

- "No" to all alcoholic beverages, such as whiskey, wine, and beer.
- "No" to drugs, tobacco, and marijuana.
- "No" to unnecessary medications like sleeping pills.
- "No" to caffeine beverages like coffee, tea, soda (Coke, Pepsi, et al.), etc.

- "No" to excess sugar in desserts.
- "No" to milk and sugar combinations.
- "No" to candy, carbonated beverages, ice cream, chewing gum, etc. which are worthless.
- "No" to spices and condiments like pepper, mustard, or anything that irritates the stomach.
- "No" to eating between meals (not even healthful things).
- "No" to unhealthful clothing or shoes.
- "No" to any habit, substance, or anything else that would harm the body.

Christians climbing the *ladder* to heaven will, with Christ's help, practice moderation in using the good things God has provided. They will totally abstain from all that is harmful. If it's bad for me, I avoid it. If it's good, I use it in moderation.

4. Rest

Do you ever wake up tired? The Creator knew exactly what He was doing when He made the sun to "rule the day" and the moon to "rule the night." He planned for men and women to get sufficient rest. David wrote, "He gives His beloved sleep" (Psalm 127:2). And Solomon says, "Yes, you will lie down and your sleep will be sweet" (Proverbs 3:24). Ideally, you should turn out your lights no later than 9:30 p. m. and get 8-10 hours of sleep every night. Then rise early and enjoy another wonderful day.

Jesus says, "Come unto Me, all you who labor and are heavy laden, and I will give you rest" (Matthew 11:28). Because He loves us, He commanded, "Six days you shall labor and do all your work, but the seventh day is the Sabbath of the Lord your God. In it you shall do no work. … For in six days the Lord made the heavens and the earth, the sea, and all that is in them, and rested the seventh day" (Exodus 20:9-11).

When God said, "Remember the Sabbath day, to keep it holy" (Exodus 20:8), He had our best interest in mind. That's why Jesus stated, "The Sabbath was made for man" (Mark 2:27).

And Paul declared, "There remains, then, a Sabbath-rest for the people of God; for anyone who enters God's rest also rests from his own work, just as God did from His" (Hebrews 4:9, 10, NIV).

Our Maker asks us to do all our work in six days and rest on the seventh. He designed the seventh day for our benefit. We can worship, rest, and relax with our families and get better acquainted with the Savior.

Jesus and His disciples got so busy, they didn't even have time to eat. Sounds like life in the 21st century! We rush here, run there, hurry, hurry, hurry, and are ready to collapse by the end of the day. Jesus says, "Come aside ... and rest a while" (Mark 6:31). Jesus went with His disciples to a deserted place. They didn't go to Disneyland. They chose a quiet place.

Everyone needs a vacation. Families are blessed by taking vacations together. Find a lonely beach, a quiet place in the mountains. Get away from the mad race and enjoy the beauty created by God Himself. Rest. Whether it's snorkeling in the sea, or backpacking in the mountains, watching a sunset, or seeing a sunrise, or standing at the top of a roaring waterfall, you will go back to your work refreshed.

5. Exercise

The most valuable exercise is useful labor outdoors. If you're a gardener or farmer, you have it made. Well, maybe. The problem is that today we have power tools and machinery to do almost everything for us. God put Adam and Eve in a garden, because He knew they needed exercise to stay strong and healthy.

After sin, God spoke saying, "In the sweat of your face you shall eat bread" (Genesis 3:19). A little perspiration is good for us. For optimum health, we need to exercise enough to make us breathe deeply and get our heart rate up.

Like too many today, my work is indoors. Too much of the time, I'm sitting in front of a computer. For exercise, my wife and I walk three miles each day. We keep it up even on rainy days, and since we live in the mountains, we walk up and down hills and manage to perspire even on cold days.

The benefits of exercise are awesome. The extra oxygen reaching our brain cells brings better thinking. Building up our heart rate and then relaxing keeps our blood pressure low. We climb in bed at night and fall asleep almost instantly. Best of all, we simply feel better.

For our vacation last summer, my wife and I backpacked into Little Yosemite in Yosemite National Park. After camping a couple of nights, we climbed Half Dome. If we weren't exercising every day, we never would have made it. On the trail, we saw teenagers who gave up before reaching the top.

Whether you're 16 or 61, you must exercise to stay alive. The view you get at the top of a mountain is worth the effort. When you reach heaven, you will rejoice to have climbed the *ladder* all the way.

6. Eat

My mother always said, "Eat to live! Don't live to eat." Scripture admonishes, "Eat ... to the glory of God" (1 Corinthians 10:31). When I get a new car, I check the manual to see what fuel and oil are recommended by the manufacturer.

Our Creator has made important recommendations regarding our diet. Jesus Himself taught us to pray, "Give us this day our daily bread" (Matthew 6:11). Wanting us to have a good diet, God says, "I have given you every herb that yields seed which is on the face of all the earth, and every tree whose fruit yields seed; to you it shall be for food" (Genesis 1:29).

Along with the perfect diet of fruits, grains, and nuts, God provided the *tree of life*. As long as Adam and Eve ate from this tree, they would live forever. But you know the story. They ate fruit from the wrong tree and lost access to the *tree of life*. With fruit from the *tree of life* no longer available, God supplemented their diet saying, "And you shall eat the herb of the field" (Genesis 3:18)."

Now the human race could eat lettuce, spinach, Swiss chard, potatoes, yams, and many other products not included in the original diet. This helped replace elements missing from the *tree of life,* but did not provide what men and women need to live forever.

When Noah faced a food shortage after the flood destroyed the earth, God permitted man to eat flesh but restricted the use of meat to clean animals as defined in Leviticus 11. The Lord also instructed, "You shall eat neither fat nor blood" (Leviticus 3:17).

With the use of flesh food, beginning at the time of Noah, the lifespan of the human race dropped dramatically from almost 1,000 years for Methuselah, to 175 for Abraham, 120 for Moses, and 70 for David. We read, "The days of our lives are seventy years" (Psalm 90:10).

God provided manna for Israel on their journey from Egypt to the Promised Land. He had "given them of the bread of heaven. Men ate angels' food" (Psalm 78:24, 25). Ungrateful, they complained and cried out, "There is nothing at all except this manna. ... Give us meat, that we may eat" (Numbers 11: 6, 13). They "lusted exceedingly in the wilderness, and tested God in the desert" (Psalm 106:14).

God sent quail by the millions. The rebellious people ate meat every day for a month. "They tested God in their heart by asking for the food of their fancy. ... He rained meat on them like the dust, feathered fowl like the sand of the seas" (Psalm 78:18, 27). "He gave them their request, but sent leanness into their soul" (Psalm 106:15). Large numbers got sick and many died. "Now these things became our examples, to the intent that we should not lust after evil things as they also lusted" (1 Corinthians 10:6).

Our loving heavenly Father provides us with the very best—fruits, grains, nuts, and vegetables. Like Israel, do we long for the fleshpots of Egypt? Are we tempted by fried chicken, cheese burger, fish and fries, or roast beef? Ask instead for a veggie-burger!

Those climbing to the top of the *ladder* will enjoy the food God provided in Eden. We will have no desire to eat dead animals, dead birds, or dead fish. Reaching heaven, we will be satisfied by the *tree of life.*

"And He showed me a pure river of water of life, clear as crystal, proceeding from the throne of God and of the Lamb. In the middle of its street, and on either side of the river, was the tree of life, which bore twelve fruits, each tree yielding its fruit every month. And the leaves of the tree were for the healing of the nations" (Revelation 22:1, 2).

How about a little heaven right now? Medical science has proved over and over that a balanced vegetarian diet adds years to our life now and gives better health. Let's eat to live!

7. Water

When I was a boy, my dad sent me out to water the horses. We watered our cow. We watered the chickens. Dad gave me a pet chipmunk saying, "Be sure and water it every day." Arriving home from church on a hot summer Sabbath, I found the chipmunk dead. Broken hearted, I realized it was my fault. I forgot to water it.

To stay alive, we need to water ourselves. Drink at least six to eight glasses a day and more when it's hot or you're involved in heavy exercise.

When they served wine to Daniel, he asked for water. Jesus promised a reward to those who serve water. "For whoever gives you a cup of water to drink … will by no means lose his reward" (Mark 9:41). But, beware! There's no reward for serving alcoholic beverages. God warns: "Woe to him who gives drink to his neighbor … to make him drunk" (Habakkuk 2:15).

The use of water is one of heaven's great blessings. We drink it. We bathe in it. We use it to wash our clothes. There's more. Hot and cold water can be very effective in treating disease. Have a headache? Try putting your feet in hot water for 20 minutes. A daily bath or shower ending with a cold shower is an excellent tonic. You want to live longer. Water!

8. Trust

Abraham Lincoln once said, "We were designed by God to trust in Him." Those who trust in divine power live longer, heal faster, and have better health. Solomon gave counsel to youth saying, "Trust in the Lord with all your heart and lean not to your own understanding. In all your ways acknowledge Him, and He shall direct your paths" (Proverbs 3:5).

"The righteous shall be glad in the Lord, and trust in Him" (Psalm 64:10). Solomon declares, "A merry [happy] heart does good, like medicine" (Proverbs 17:22). David could say, "For You are my hope, O Lord God; You are my trust from my youth" (Psalm 71:5).

Trust will lead us to pray. Jesus said, "Men always ought to pray and not to lose heart" (Luke 18:1). Paul wrote, "We trust in the living God" (1 Timothy 4:10). He promises, "I am the Lord who heals you" (Exodus 15:26). There's a condition to this promise: "If you diligently heed the voice of the Lord your God and do what is right in His sight" (Exodus 15:26).

Trust is faith in Jesus. Troubled hearts create broken bodies. The Savior says, "Let not your heart be troubled; you believe in God, believe also in Me" (John 14:1).

Five verses later He reminds us, saying, "I am the way" (John 14:6). He is the *ladder*. We climb with Him. *Temperance* is a very important step on the *ladder*. Our "body is the temple of the Holy Spirit. ... For you were bought at a price; therefore glorify God in your body and in your spirit, which are God's" (1 Corinthians 6:19, 20).

"Put on the Lord Jesus Christ, and make no provision for the flesh, to fulfill its lusts" (Romans 13:14). "Whatever you do, do all to the glory of God" (1 Corinthians 10:31).

Jesus loves us and desires the very best for us always. "Beloved, I pray that you may prosper in all things and be in health" (3 John 2).

Temperance means developing right habits. Those who trust in God and practice *temperance* have much to look forward to. "For the trumpet will sound, and the dead will be raised incorruptible, and we shall be changed. For this corruptible must put on incorruption, and this mortal must put on immortality. ... Thanks be to God who gives us the victory through our Lord Jesus Christ" (1 Corinthians 15:52, 53, 57).

I will live a life of TEMPERANCE,
Jesus give me strength.

Points to Remember
1. Jesus offers the abundant life to give us joy, health and eternal life.
2. We honor Jesus by taking the best possible care of our bodies.
3. *Temperance* is self-control. We choose what is best and totally abstain from all that is harmful.
4. Jesus gives us power to say "No" to alcohol, tobacco, drugs, caffeine and all other harmful substances.
5. The best beverage is water.
6. Practicing *temperance* in all things is a response of love for our Creator.

Climb Higher

God Offers Temperance
"If you will walk in obedience to His will, learning cheerfully and diligently the lessons of His providence, . . . He will say, 'Child, come up higher to the heavenly mansions which I have prepared for you" (*Our High Calling*, 261).

"Faith, virtue, science, *temperance*, [are rounds] of the *ladder*. We are saved by climbing round after round, mounting step after step, to the height of Christ's ideal for us" (Translated from *Los Hechos de los Apostoles*, 422. Compare with *The Acts of the Apostles*, 530).

The Ladder
"**If the youth today** would stand as Daniel stood, they must put to the stretch every spiritual nerve and muscle. The Lord ... desires them to reach the very highest round of the *ladder* that they may step from it into the kingdom of God" (Ellen G. White, *The Youth's Instructor*, July 27, 1899).

Temperance

"Everyone who competes for the prize is *temperate* in all things. Now they do it to obtain a perishable crown, but we for an imperishable crown" (1 Corinthians 9:25).

"**The health** should be as faithfully guarded as the character" (*Messages to Young People*, 232).

"***Temperance* is a round of the *ladder*.** ... In food, in raiment, in work, in regular hours, in healthful exercise, we must be regulated by the knowledge which it is our duty to obtain that we may ... place ourselves in right relation to life and health" (*Our High Calling*, 65).

"**True** *temperance* teaches us to dispense entirely with everything hurtful and to use judiciously that which is healthful" (*Patriarchs and Prophets*, 562).

"***Pure air, sunlight, abstemiousness, rest, exercise, proper diet, the use of water, trust in divine power***—these are the true remedies" (*The Ministry of Healing*, 127).

1. Pure Air

"The Lord, ... who spread forth the earth ... gives breath to the people on it" (Isaiah 42:5).

"**In order to have good blood**, we must breathe well. Full, deep inspirations of pure air which fill the lungs with oxygen, purify the blood. They impart to it a bright color, and send it, a life-giving current, to every part of the body. A good respiration soothes the nerves; it stimulates the appetite and renders digestion more perfect; and it induces sound, refreshing sleep" (*The Ministry of Healing*, 272).

2. Sunlight

"You have prepared the light and the sun" (Psalm 74:16).

"**Have your home as attractive as you can have it.** Put back the drapery and let heaven's doctor in, which is sunlight" (*Temperance*, 209).

3. Abstemiousness

"Abstain from fleshly lusts" (1 Peter 2:11).

"**Let Christ's followers abstain** not only from alcohol, tobacco, tea, and coffee, but also from every other harmful thing that beclouds the brain" (*Sermons and Talks*, 2:196).

"**The Bible** nowhere sanctions the use of intoxicating wine" (*The Ministry of Healing*, 333).

"**Tea acts as a stimulant**, and, to a certain extent, produces intoxication. The action of coffee and many other popular drinks is similar" (*The Ministry of Healing*, 325).

4. Rest

"I will give you rest" (Matthew 11:28).

"**We must take periods of rest**, periods of recreation, periods for contemplation. . . . Recreation in the open air, the contemplation of the works of God in nature, will be of the highest benefit" (*The Faith I Live By*, 233).

5. Exercise

"Six days you shall labor and do all your work" (Exodus 20:9).

"**Action is a law of our being**. … The normal action of all the organs gives strength and vigor, while the tendency of disuse is toward decay and death" (*The Ministry of Healing*, 237).

"The best thing most of us can do, say the experts, may be to walk. … Walking, in fact, may be the perfect exercise" (Christine Gorman, "Walk, Don't Run," *Time*, January 21, 2002).

6. Proper Diet

"Put a knife to your throat if you are a man given to appetite" (Proverbs 23:2).

"**It is impossible** for those who indulge the appetite to attain to Christian perfection" (*Counsels on Diet and Foods*, 22).

"**Grains, fruits, nuts, and vegetables** constitute the diet chosen for us by our Creator. These foods, prepared in as simple and natural a manner as possible, are the most healthful and nourishing"(*The Ministry of Healing*, 296).

"**Flesh** was never the best food; but its use is now doubly objectionable, since disease in animals is so rapidly increasing" (*The Ministry of Healing*, 313).

7. The Use of Water

"Let me drink a little water" (Genesis 24:17).

"Pure water is one of heaven's choicest blessings. Its proper use promotes health. It is the beverage which God provided. … Drunk freely, it helps to supply the necessities of the system and assists nature to resist disease. The external application of water is one of the easiest … ways of regulating the circulation of the blood. A cold or cool bath is an excellent tonic. Warm baths open the pores and thus aid in the elimination of impurities. Both warm and neutral baths soothe the nerves and equalize the circulation" (*The Ministry of Healing*, 237).

8. Trust in Divine Power

"Commit your way to the Lord, Trust also in Him" (Psalm 37:5).

"**Courage, hope, faith, sympathy, love, promote health** and prolong life. A contented mind, a cheerful spirit, is health to the body and strength to the soul" (*The Ministry of Healing*, 241).

"**Many of the diseases** from which men suffer are the result of mental depression. Grief, anxiety, discontent, remorse, guilt, distrust, all tend to break down the life forces and to invite decay and death" (*The Ministry of Healing*, 241).

"**Let your heart trust in God.** Place your confidence in Him. His hand sustains you, and if you abide in Christ, you will grow stronger and stronger" (*Daughters of God*, 185).

Chapter 6
Fly Your Flag!

Jesus proclaims, *"I am the WAY, the truth and the life.*
No one comes to the Father except through me."
—John 14:6

We are saved by climbing with Jesus.
Steps up the *ladder* include faith, science,
temperance, and PATIENCE

ow much longer do I have to wait? I wondered. *If only I could have a driver's license now!*

Teenagers today would say I was actually very lucky, because I got my first driver's license when I was 14. I had started driving off-road on the farm when I was seven, so I'd been waiting impatiently for half of my life.

Six years later, when I was 20, I graduated from college and received my first assignment as a young minister. "You will need to have a chauffeur's license," a letter from a church administrator advised. I soon learned why.

The new professional chauffeur's license in my billfold qualified me to drive a truck or bus. A youth director called, saying, "We have arranged for Camp Wawona to use the Dinuba Junior Academy bus for the summer, and we want you to be the driver."

I'll never forget my first trip to camp. A dozen girls boarded the bus in Dinuba. I started the engine and let out the clutch. We were off. I shifted gears smoothly. At 35 miles an hour, the bus began to vibrate. *This thing will shake apart before we get to Fresno*, I imagined. At 50 miles an hour, the vibration stopped.

A crowd of girls, with lots of luggage, waited at the old O Street Church as I crammed their baggage into every possible spot. When the last girl boarded, I had 47 campers packed in on board a bus designed to hold 35. *Oh, well, this isn't too bad,* I thought. When I attended Junior Camp, they loaded us like animals into the back of a truck, but we didn't care. It added to the excitement.

Before pulling away from the church on a very hot morning, I asked a counselor to pray. She asked Jesus to watch over the bus and take us safely all the way to camp.

We started up the first hill on Highway 41 heading into the mountains. Then bang! I looked at the temperature gauge—212° Fahrenheit. *Oh, no! The engine's overheated!* I pulled off to the side of the road and jumped out to check. Lifting the hood, I saw the trouble. The generator had dropped off its mount on the side of the engine and lay at the bottom of the motor. And no fan belt! *I guess it fell off and is lost.*

Back on the bus, I explained to the girls. "We have a problem. The engine is too hot to start and I'm afraid to try to coast back down the hill to a service station with anyone in the bus." I put a counselor in charge and asked the girls to stay in the shade of a big oak tree and stay off the road.

I waited until there was no traffic coming in either direction and let off the brake. The big yellow bus began to roll backwards. I crossed to the other side of the road and coasted into the service station. A mechanic saw me coming and came out. "What can I do for you? he asked.

"Sir, I'm praying you will have the right bolts to remount the generator, and I need a new fan belt to replace the one lost when the generator fell off."

"I wouldn't count on it," he said.
He started looking through a drawer full of old bolts. "You are really fortunate. Here's exactly what you need." He had the right tools and in minutes the generator was in place. "I don't know about finding the right size fan belt." He began to search. I kept praying.

Soon he came back smiling. "This is the only truck fan belt we have in stock." Putting it on, he said, "I'm amazed. It's exactly the right size." We also added water to the radiator. I paid for the service, started the engine, and pulled back out onto the highway.

Reaching the oak, I stopped to let the 47 girls climb back onto the bus. "God is really good to us," I said. "The service station had everything we needed to get us back on the road."

"Now we're going to get to camp late," one girl complained. I totally agreed when she said, "I sure hope we don't have any more problems."

Back on the highway, the old yellow bus charged ahead. I tried to keep it under 35 or over 50, so we wouldn't have the shakes. Otherwise, everything was fine. We reached 3,000 feet elevation, crossed over the pass, and dropped into the valley.

But soon, we began climbing more, and I shifted into lower gears. Before reaching 5,000 feet, we inched up a steep grade in second gear. Suddenly the engine stopped! *Now what's going on?* I worried.

Quickly I turned toward the edge of the highway, and the bus stopped. I hit the brakes to keep from rolling backwards. The brake pedal went all the way to the floorboard. *No brakes!* I managed to cram the gear into low and pulled the emergency brake. We were safely stopped, but outside the rear window I heard a shrill, whistling sound. *Oh, no! The rear tire's going flat!* I crawled under the bus and discovered the problem: The air hose had fallen across the exhaust pipe and burned a hole in it. *There's no way I can fix this,* I thought to myself. *At least I can put on the spare tire.*

"Girls," I announced. "We are going to jack up the bus and change the tire. We need you to get out and stand off the highway in the shade on the other side of the road." We stopped traffic from both directions and helped the girls cross the highway safely.

Jacking up the bus proved difficult because we were parked against a ridge of dirt. I loosened the wheel nuts, and with the dual rear wheels finally raised off the ground, I went ahead and removed them. *One blessing,* I thought. *The flat tire is on the outside.*

I gripped the large truck tire and began pulling. Nothing happened. I jacked the wheel a little higher. I struggled, but the big wheel still wouldn't come off. I cleaned out some of the dirt on the edge of the bank. It didn't help.

A girl on the other side of the road said, "It's sure taking a long time to change the tire."

Another girl asked, "How are we ever going to get to camp? Our bus driver doesn't even know how to change a tire."
Sweat flowed as I pulled harder. The wheel refused to budge. *Guess the girl's right. I've never changed a truck tire before. They didn't tell me how to do this when I got my chauffeur's license. I really do need to get back on the road and get these girls to camp.* I really couldn't see what I was doing, and desperate to get going again, I dropped to my knees. Closing my eyes I prayed, "Lord, I need your help."

Still on my knees, I reached down under the hub where I couldn't see. My fingers touched another nut. *How could I be so stupid? No wonder the wheel doesn't come off.* I stopped and counted—exactly 10 wheel nuts. I'd taken off only nine! I picked up the wrench and removed nut number 10. Taking the big wheel in my hands, I pulled. It slid off so easy. "Thank you, Lord," I prayed. "Help me remember this. You gave us 10 commandments—10 ways to love. Breaking one commandment—one unconfessed sin, will keep me from escaping this old world and going to my home in heaven."

It's true. "Blessed are those who do His commandments, that they may … enter through the gates into the city" (Revelation 22:14, KJV).

In minutes, I had the spare tire on and the engine running. Stopping traffic again, I helped the girls cross back over the highway and into the bus. I didn't tell anyone that we didn't have brakes. "Lord, I need your help more than ever. I'm going to go slow and stay in lower gears. The emergency brake isn't worth much."

We managed to stop at the entrance to Yosemite National Park. Hearing the magic words, "Camp Wawona," the ranger waved us on. We crept down the long grade ahead, staying in low gear all the way. Two miles from camp, we left the main highway and turned right up a narrow road. We started up a little rise. Boom! The girls screamed. "Now what's going on?"

The temperature gauge jumped back to the top! The over-heated engine died. We were stopped in the shade, so I left my passengers in the bus. A quick look under the hood revealed the problem. The radiator hose had popped off and all the water leaked out.

I walked to the nearest house, borrowed a screwdriver, a pair of pliers, and a bucket. The tools were just what I needed to reinstall the radiator hose. I used the bucket to get water from the river to fill the radiator.

After returning the tools and bucket, we drove on, nearly clipping off our outside mirrors as we squeezed between giant trees. Arriving at camp, I used the emergency brake and low gear to come to a safe stop. The girls sang at the top of their voices, "Our camp in the fair Sierras, 'neath the old Wawona Dome."

I opened the door and watched 47 tired, happy campers climb off the bus. One girl looked up saying, "It sure takes a lot of *patience* to ride in and old bus like this." I thought, *And it takes more patience to drive an old bus like this.* I was glad that before starting out, we had stopped and prayed placing our faith in Jesus. And the 10 wheel nuts—God wants us to love Him and obey all 10 of His commandments.

It all comes together in one short verse. "Here is the *patience* of the saints; here are those who keep the commandments of God and the faith of Jesus" (Revelation 14:12). *Patience*, obedience, faith! David says, "You have given a banner to those who fear You, that it may be displayed because of the truth" (Psalm 60:4).

Our banner, our flag, displays *patience,* obedience, and faith. *Patience* is a very important step on the *ladder* to heaven. *Patience* is one of my greatest needs. God's word speaks directly to me, "For you have need of *patience*" (Hebrews 10:36, KJV). Why do I need patience? The Bible explains, "So that after you have done the will of God, you may receive the promise" (Hebrews 10:36).

The promise is a home in heaven. I need *patience* to get there. An unknown author lists four items that help me understand what *patience* is all about:

1. Bearing pains or trials calmly or without complaint.
2. Manifesting forbearance under provocation or strain.
3. Not being hasty or impetuous.
4. Remaining steadfast despite opposition, difficulty, or adversity.

I look at this list and ask, "Do I measure up?" The answer is "No! I have a hot temper. I get angry. I lose *patience* with my family—my wife, my children, sometimes even with my friends. I've even been impatient with myself. What am I going to do?"

I must cling to Jesus and keep on climbing with Him. God gave me the power of choice. I can choose to be patient. My Webster's Dictionary defines *patience* as "the habit of being patient." I can surrender my will to Jesus and ask Him to help me be patient. He has promised to work in me. "For it is God who works in you both to will and to do His good pleasure" (Philippians 2:13). When I climb the *ladder* with Jesus, He helps me form the habit of being patient.

Years ago my wife and I climbed Mount Nebo and looked across the lush Jordan Valley toward the *Promised Land.* Our minds flooded with memories of Bible stories we'd read since childhood. Some 35 centuries earlier, Moses, at 120, walked alone up this same mountain.

Moses listened patiently to the complaints of Israel for 40 years. Near the beginning of their journey, they lacked water and God asked Moses to strike the rock. Water gushed out. In all their wilderness wanderings, wherever they camped, they drank water from the rock. Jesus is not only the Rock, He is the Living Water. His grace brings us salvation. He alone can make us patient.

As they neared the end of the journey, water ceased to flow, and the children of Israel began to complain. Moses lost his *patience*. Instead of speaking to the rock, as God commanded, he struck the rock twice. Water flowed and grateful people drank, but Moses failed to honor God.

In a moment of impatience, Moses asked, "Must we bring water for you out of this rock?" (Numbers 20:10). "We?" Impossible! Only the Creator could make water flow from the rock, and Moses failed to give Him credit.

The Lord said, "You will not cross the Jordan." One sin kept a great leader from reaching the Promised Land. My impatience can keep me from reaching the top of the *ladder!* So I pray for *patience*. And you know what happens? Every time I pray for *patience*, I have more problems. My whole life has been like the bus trip to camp in Yosemite National Park. Problems! Problems! More problems!

Shall I lower the banner? Shall I give up? Shall I stop climbing? I must take courage and cling to the *ladder*. I must listen to the Holy Spirit when He speaks to me. Even when I fail to be patient, it's no time to give up the struggle. I must resolve to be more firm in resisting my natural inclinations. I must look to Jesus as the one who can help me calmly face every provocation.

Moses took things into his own hands when he killed the Egyptian. God gave him 40 years herding sheep to learn *patience*. During the next 40 years, Moses demonstrated remarkable *patience* in dealing with the Israelites. But even Moses lost his cool. His *patience* failed. "Hear now, you rebels!" he shouted. His accusation was true, but even truth needs to be spoken without passion or impatience.

Impatient words destroy families. Uncontrolled temper leads to divorce. Impatience causes children to rebel against parents. Failure to climb the step of *patience* will keep us from reaching the top of the *ladder*. Lack of *patience* at the end of a long, hard journey cost Moses the privilege of entering the Promised Land with the chosen people of God.

Moses, 120 years old, confessed his sin and prayed for pardon. With a broken heart, he spoke to the people, "I must die in this land, I must not cross over the Jordan" (Deuteronomy 4:22). He reviewed the 10 commandments and pointed out the importance of loving God and doing His will.

Then alone Moses climbed Mt. Nebo. He met the Lord and received a panoramic view of the Promised Land. Often referred to as the most patient man who ever lived, He lay down in the mysterious stillness of the mountain and died. Angels buried him in a lonely grave.

Moses lost his *patience*. Most of us have lost our *patience* many more times than he did. Jesus calls us to patiently climb the *ladder* until we reach the top and step into His kingdom. Because Moses learned the lesson of *patience*, his time in the grave was short. Christ and the angels returned from heaven to resurrect a sleeping saint. For the very first time Jesus gave life to one who had died. Satan, who contested this act of Christ, learned that the righteous dead will live again.

By not allowing Moses to enter Canaan, God teaches that He requires *patience*, complete obedience, and faith. We must never take to ourselves the credit that belongs to Him. A gracious God recognized the loving service of Moses, forgave his sin, and called him to a reward infinitely greater than the land of Canaan. He inherited heaven.

Standing with my wife, Evelyn, on top of Mount Nebo, we remembered how Jesus left heaven itself, came to this earth, and with *patience* suffered far more than we will ever suffer. He died on the cross to give us eternal life. We prayed asking God for Christ-like *patience*.

Jesus is coming soon! It's time to fly our flag and keep it high. We must say with the Psalmist, "We will rejoice in your salvation, and in the name of our God we will set up our banners!" (Psalm 20:5). Our banner, our flag, declares *patience*, obedience, and faith. "Let us run with *patience* the race that is set before us, Looking unto Jesus the author and finisher of our faith" (Hebrews 12:1, 2, KJV).

We must pray for "a walk worthy of the Lord, fully pleasing Him, being fruitful in every good work and increasing in the knowledge of God; strengthened with all might, according to His glorious power, for all *patience* and longsuffering with joy" (Colossians 1:10, 11).

We don't climb the *ladder* to impress God. That's legalism. We climb the *ladder* to please God. That's love. Each step of the way, we receive His righteousness by faith. The words inscribed on our flag say, "Here is the *patience* of the saints; here are those who keep the commandments of God and the faith of Jesus" (Revelation 14:12). "In the name of our God, we will set up our banners" (Psalm 20:5).

Climbing with Jesus, fly your flag high! Higher! Show the world that *patience* is possible when we cling to Christ. *Patience* and obedience result from faith in Jesus.

I will pray each day for PATIENCE,
Make me more like Christ.

Points to Remember

1. We all need more *patience.*
2. *Patience* is a habit we need to cultivate daily.
3. Living to impress God is legalism.
4. Pleasing God is love.
5. We receive His righteousness by faith.
6. God allows trials and perplexities to develop our *patience.*

Climb Higher

God Offers Patience

"We want a daily renewal of the grace of God in our hearts, that we may climb the *ladder* of perfection step by step, rising higher and higher in the way that leads to heaven, to holiness, and to God" (*Review and Herald*, May 18, 1905).

"Faith, virtue, science, temperance, *patience*, ... [are rounds] of the *ladder*. We are saved by climbing round after round, mounting step after step, to the height of Christ's ideal for us" (Translated from *Los Hechos de los Apostoles*, 422. Compare with *The Acts of the Apostles*, 530).

"Let *patience*, gratitude, and love keep sunshine in the heart" (*The Adventist Home*, 18).

The Ladder

"**Will we *patiently* climb the *ladder*** of Christian progress, until from the top-most round we step into the kingdom of our Lord Jesus Christ?" (*Signs of the Times*, October 22, 1885).

"**Not in your own strength**, but in the strength of Christ, you are to ascend the *ladder* heavenward" (*Letters from Ellen G. White to Sanitarium Workers in Southern California*, 4).

"**Character will be tested**. ... We shall be *patient*, kind, and forbearing, cheerful amid frets and irritations. Day by day and year by year we shall conquer self and grow into a noble heroism. This is our allotted task; but it cannot be accomplished without continual help from Jesus, resolute decision, unwavering purpose, continual watchfulness, and unceasing prayer. Each one has a personal battle to fight. ... Those who decline the struggle lose the strength and joy of victory. No one, not even God, can carry us to heaven unless we make the necessary effort on our part" (*Testimonies for the Church*, 5:345).

Patience

Our goal is to have the patience of Jesus: "Count it all joy when you fall into various trials, knowing that the testing of your faith produces *patience*" (James 1:2, 3).

"**Though you so often fail to reveal** *patience* **and** calmness, do not give up the struggle. Resolve again, this time more firmly, to be patient under every provocation. And never take your eyes off your divine Example" (*Messages to Young People*, 135).

"**To wait patiently in hope** when clouds envelop us and all is dark, requires faith and submission which causes our will to be swallowed up in the will of God. We are too quickly discouraged, and earnestly cry for the trial to be removed from us, when we should plead for *patience* to endure and grace to overcome" (*Testimonies for the Church*, 1:310).

"**When impatient words are spoken** to you, do not retaliate. Words spoken in reply to the one who is angry usually act as a whip, lashing the temper into greater fury. But anger met by silence quickly dies away. Let the Christian bridle his tongue, firmly resolving not to speak harsh, impatient words. … In his own strength man cannot rule his spirit. But through Christ he may gain self-control. … The religion of Christ brings the emotions under the control of reason and disciplines the tongue. Under its influence the hasty temper is subdued, and the heart is filled with *patience* and gentleness" (*Messages to Young People*, 135, 136).

Our Flag

"**God has placed in our hands a banner** upon which is inscribed, 'Here is the *patience* of the saints; here are they that keep the commandments of God, and the faith of Jesus'" (*Testimonies for the Church*, 7:150).

"**Watch the banner of our holy faith,** and be found where that waves, even though it be in the thickest of the fight. … If you are faithful you will come off more than conquerors through Him that has loved you" (*Testimonies for the Church*, 5:309).

Chapter 7
Mummy
in the Museum

Jesus proclaims, *"I am the WAY, the truth and the life.*
No one comes to the Father except through me."
—John 14:6

We are saved by climbing with Jesus.
Steps up the *ladder* include faith, science,
temperance, patience, and PIETY.

"*G*old, gold, and more gold!" my wife exclaimed. We marveled at the awesome treasures of Tutankhamen on display inside the Cairo Museum, located on the banks of the Nile River. The King Tut exhibition contains entire rooms filled with objects from his tomb. A boat for sailing on the Nile was an artifact that caught my attention. Imagine being buried with your boat! We saw hundreds of other items designed for luxurious living.

But more than anything else—fabulous amounts of gold. Two outer coffins were covered with gold. Pharaoh Tutankhamen's inner coffin was made of solid gold. The beauty of the dazzling gold facemask sent shivers up our spines. *Encyclopedia Britannica* claims this is the largest collection of gold and jewelry in the world today.

A college classmate, serving as a missionary in Egypt, had driven us through impossible traffic on crowded streets of the Middle East's largest city. "Now," he nudged us. "We need to get going. I want to show you the mummy room before it closes."

Case after glass case contained mummies of Egyptian pharaohs. We looked at well-preserved remains thousands of years old. Our guide pointed to one mummy. "Many believe this is the 'stiff-necked pharaoh' who refused to let Israel go." *If that's true,* I thought, *he must have washed ashore after being drowned in the Red Sea. Perhaps he was carried back and embalmed.* I got permission to take a picture. This pharaoh really does look like he has a stiff neck.

We were led to another mummy. "This one could have been Moses," our guide said. *Moses?* I wondered. *Moses died alone on Mount Nebo. Angels buried him in an unknown grave. Moses is not a mummy!*

The next day we were dropped off at the Cairo airport. As our family flew back across the Mediterranean to Athens, I had time to think more about our exciting visit to the Cairo Museum. Moses, adopted by Pharaoh's daughter, could have inherited the riches of Egypt.

Where is Moses anyway? The last chapter of Deuteronomy tells us he was buried in a valley in the land of Moab and no one knows the location of his grave. My friend had pointed to a mummy saying, "This could have been Moses." Why isn't Moses in the Cairo Museum?

The Bible gives just enough information to solve the mystery. "Yet Michael the archangel, in contending with the devil … disputed about the body of Moses" (Jude 9). You see, a dispute took place over the body of Moses, but who is Michael? He's mentioned three times in Daniel and also in Revelation 12:7. Each time, this being is in conflict with Satan.

By comparing Scripture with Scripture, we discover that Michael is Christ. Jude refers to Michael as the archangel, one who is over the angels. Speaking of the coming of Jesus, Paul declares, "For the Lord Himself will descend from heaven with a shout, with the voice of an archangel, and with the trumpet of God. And the dead in Christ will rise first" (1 Thessalonians 4:16).

Jesus said, "Most assuredly, I say to you, the hour is coming … when the dead will hear the voice of the Son of God; and those who hear will live. … Do not marvel at this; for the hour is coming in which all who are in the graves will hear His voice" (John 5:25, 28).

The Bible is clear:

1. Michael is the archangel.
2. The archangel calls the dead to rise at the second coming.
3. The voice of Jesus, the Son of God, calls the dead, so Jesus is Michael the archangel.

This means that Jesus and the devil disputed over the body of Moses! We know who won because it was Moses who came down with Elijah on the Mount of Transfiguration. Moses is alive! Moses is in heaven. Jesus won in the contest with Satan.

Let's imagine what happened when Jesus came to raise Moses from the dead. The Devil says, "Sorry, you can't have him. He killed an Egyptian. You told him to speak to the rock. He lost his patience and disobeyed by striking the rock. He's mine."

Jesus may have reminded Satan, "You tempted Moses to commit murder. You're the one who wore down his patience by continually leading the Israelites to complain and rebel."

Satan glares at Jesus. "You said that all who disobey, must die. You have no right to resurrect Moses."

Jesus says, "I kept Moses out of the Promised Land to teach a lesson never to be forgotten. God requires exact obedience."

"Then I'm right," Satan declares. "He disobeyed. You have no right to bring him back to life."

"Remember, Satan," Jesus answers. "I was ready to destroy Israel. I even promised to make Moses a great nation. He is like me. He offered to die for his people. He asked me to blot his name from the Book of Life and save Israel. I will come and die on a cross to save him."

The devil snarls, "You're telling me that Moses was a good man?"

"I'm saying that Moses is a sinner saved by grace. You've delayed me long enough. Please step back, Satan," Jesus commanded.

"Moses, come!" Jesus called. "I'm taking you to heaven right now."

For the very first time ever recorded, Jesus gave life to the dead. God remembered the *piety*, humility, forbearance and Moses' supreme love to God. The Lord did not grant His request to enter the earthly Canaan. He gave him something much better—an entrance into the everlasting Kingdom of Jesus Christ. Instead of being a dead mummy, Moses is alive in heaven.

Piety is another step on the *ladder* to heaven. *Piety* or godliness deals with lifestyle or conduct. *Webster's Collegiate Dictionary* suggests that *piety* is "the quality or state of being pious." It's "fidelity to natural obligations, dutifulness in religion, a belief or standard."

Standard? Nobody likes standards. But wait, Jesus is the standard. Humanity linked with divinity results in *piety*. It means being like Jesus. It's righteousness by faith. Moses, more than any other man on earth, became like Christ.

Enoch before him, and Elijah after him, climbed to the top of the *ladder* without seeing death. Moses was the first to die and be raised to reach heaven at the top of the *ladder*. Why isn't Moses a mummy in the Cairo Museum? Paul provides the answer.

"By faith Moses, when he became of age, refused to be called the son of Pharaoh's daughter, choosing rather to suffer affliction with the people of God than to enjoy the passing pleasures of sin, esteeming the reproach of Christ greater riches than the treasures in Egypt; for he looked to the reward. By faith he forsook Egypt" (Hebrews 11:24-27).

God in His providence allowed Howard Carter to discover King Tut's tomb back in 1922. His sensational discovery in Egypt's Valley of the Kings helps youth living now, when Jesus is about to return, to understand the choice Moses made and the choice we must make in order to reach the top of the *ladder*.

Archeologists and historians claim that Tutankhamen was one of the poorer kings of Egypt. Yet the contents of his tomb reveal a sensual and luxurious lifestyle hardly matched even by the wealthiest today. The kingdom by the Nile offered the world's most pleasing pleasures. Pharaohs had access to the most expensive alcoholic beverages, the finest and tastiest food, attractive music, and seductive women. Dance, drama, and theater provided never-ending entertainment. Possessions of gold and the world's finest jewelry prompted pride.

Snatched from a basket floating on the Nile, and adopted by Pharaoh's daughter, Moses could have become head of the greatest empire on earth. The Bible says he "refused to become the son of Pharaoh's daughter." All the "pleasures of sin" were his to enjoy. He chose instead to "suffer affliction with the people of God." The wealth of Egypt was his to inherit. He chose the "reproach of Christ" as "greater riches than the [fabulous] treasures of Egypt."

Why? "He looked to the reward." Providence allowed Moses to spend his first 12 years with his Hebrew parents. Over and over, he heard stories that had been passed from father to son, stories he would later be inspired to record for all time in the book of Genesis. As a youth, he learned about Jacob and the *ladder* to heaven. Before going to live in Pharaoh's palace, he determined that more than anything else, he wanted to reach the top of the *ladder*.

There's pleasure in sin. Don't let anyone tell you there isn't. The problem is—it doesn't last. Moses knew that Pharaohs became mummies. He believed that with the Savior, he could have eternal life. The wise man is up front with the issue. "As righteousness *leads* to life, so he who pursues evil pursues it to his own death" (Proverbs 11:19). Moses "looked to the reward. He forsook Egypt." He could have been a mummy in a museum. His choice to forsake the pleasures of sin and the treasures of Egypt, put him in heaven.

Moses, at 120 years of age, appealed to God's people saying, "I have set before you life and death. ... Choose life, that both you and your descendants may live; that you may love the Lord your God, that you may obey His voice, and that you may cling to Him" (Deuteronomy 30:19, 20).

We can cling to the *ladder*. We can pray, "Teach me to do Your will" (Psalm 143:10). Moses' *piety* led him to make the right choice. He forsook the pleasures of this world. Three texts demand the careful attention of all who seek to be like Jesus and climb the *ladder* to heaven.

1. "Do not be conformed to this world, but be transformed by the renewing of your mind, that you may prove what is that good and acceptable and perfect will of God" (Romans 12:2).
2. "Do not love the world or the things in the world. If anyone loves the world, the love of the Father is not in him. For all that is in the world—the lust of the flesh, the lust of the eyes, and the pride of life—is not of the Father but is of the world. And the world is passing away, and the lust of it; but he who does the will of God abides forever" (1 John 2:15-17).
3. "Enter by the narrow gate; for wide is the gate and broad is the way that leads to destruction, and there are many who go in by it. Because narrow is the gate and difficult is the way which leads to life, and there are few who find it" (Matthew 7:13, 14).

The Bible is very clear. Culture is not the basis for right or wrong. We are to seek the "good and acceptable and perfect will of God." God spoke to Moses saying, "According to the doings of the land of Egypt, where you dwelt, you shall not do; and according to the doings of the land of Canaan, where I am bringing you, you shall not do" (Leviticus 18:3).

What are the things of this world? I've asked this question to teenagers around the globe. Youth who study their Bibles, although living in different cultures, come up with about the same answers. Here are just a few of the worldly things they put on their list:

- Amusement Parks & Arcades
- Carnivals & Circuses
- Casinos & Gambling
- Dancing & Partying
- Discotheques & Nightclubs
- Movies & Theater
- TV & Video Games
- Internet's evil sites
- Jazz, Swing, Rock Music
- Makeup & Jewelry
- Immodest Dress & Pornography
- Commercial Sport & Card Playing

Paul looked forward to our time when he wrote, "In the last days perilous times will come; for men will be lovers ... of pleasure rather than lovers of God, having a form of *[piety]* but denying its power" (2 Timothy 3:1, 2, 4, 5).

Piety, or being like Jesus, is a missing element in too many lives today. Some argue saying, "We don't need a bunch of rules. It's time to revise our old-fashioned standards." Let's review a standard inspired by Jesus: "Whatever things are true, whatever things are noble, whatever things are just, whatever things are pure, whatever things are lovely, whatever things are of good report, if there is any virtue and if there is anything praiseworthy—meditate [think] on these things" (Philippians 4:8). Would you want to change this rule?

Paul wrote to Timothy saying, "Be strong in the grace that is in Christ Jesus. ... If anyone competes in athletics, he is not crowned unless he competes according to the rules" (2 Timothy 2:1, 5). Those who seek a crown of life in God's eternal kingdom find joy in living by the rules. "Do not love the world or the things in the world" is a safe rule to follow.

It would take another book to deal with all the ins and outs, whys and wherefores of even a partial list of worldly practices and places in our time. Let's look at just one item. You can take the principle of living to please Jesus and study the rest for yourself. For Moses it was the pleasures of Egypt or heaven. Could it be that, for you and me, it's Hollywood or heaven?

What is God's will regarding cinema? This includes the entire Hollywood-based film industry—theater, movies, videos, DVDs, television, MTV, and many things available on the World Wide Web. Hollywood entertainment displays about every sinful pleasure known to man. It's true, "By beholding, we become changed."

On two occasions, youth serving on a church nominating committee objecting to a name recommended for church office because of movies they had seen in the members' home. They have a point. Hollywood sells sin. It exists to make big bucks. Our Christian mission is to help people reach God's kingdom.

One church's official position on movies affirms: "We are called to be a godly people who think, feel, and act in harmony with the principles of heaven. ... Our amusement and entertainment should meet the highest standards of Christian taste and beauty. ... Radio and television ... bring ... almost continuous theatrical performances and many influences that are neither wholesome nor uplifting. ... We earnestly warn against the *subtle and sinister influence of the moving-picture theater*, which is no place for the Christian. ... Shun those places of amusement and those theatrical films that glorify professional acting and actors. ... Let us not patronize the commercialized amusements, joining with the worldly, careless, pleasure-loving multitudes. ... In the Christian life there is complete separation from worldly practices, such as card playing, theater going, dancing, et cetera."

A Christian's consistent conduct builds church credibility. Why is attendance growing in the churches where youth spoke out against movies? And why did tithe increase almost 50 percent in less than three years in those same churches? We asked one church leader. He says, "It's because our church is trying to uphold Jesus and His standards."

A religious academy's high school senior class voted to spend class night at a movie theater. Some students, convicted by the

Holy Spirit, said they couldn't go. They wanted to do something special and phoned a former mission pilot. That night they took an exciting flight over their city and learned more about mission aviation. The other students said the movie was lousy. Solomon counsels, "If sinners entice you, Do not consent. ... Do not walk in the way with them, Keep your foot from their path; for their feet run to evil" (Proverbs 1:10, 15, 16).

We need to let Scripture principles guide us in what we watch. Those who accept the gift of Christ's righteousness say, "I will set nothing wicked before my eyes" (Psalm 101:3). God instructed, "Each of you, throw away the abominations which are before his eyes" (Ezekiel 20:7).

Flee the horrors of Hollywood. Jesus said, "If your eye is bad, your whole body will be full of darkness" (Matthew 6:23). Observe sin and you will serve Satan. "Turn your eyes upon Jesus" and you'll be like Him. Remember, "Do not love the world. ... The lust of the eyes, and the pride of life is not of the Father" (1 John 2:15, 16).

I baptized a young woman who grew up in a religious home. She said, "There is hardly one good movie in a hundred." Teenagers in my church say, "Even if you find a good movie at a theater, you will still see questionable previews." Hollywood markets sin. You wouldn't go to a bar to buy milk for a baby. Theater attendance may wrongly influence others. You may get into the movie habit yourself and be led away from Jesus.

Selectivity seldom works. Consistent Christians choose not to watch bad movies at home or school or even in a church social hall. They live to honor Jesus by what they see, hear, and where they go. They allow the attractions in nature to provide recreation.

Christ once commented, "The children of this world ... are wiser than the children of light" (Luke 16:8). Many wise, and discriminating, in the world recognize serious problems even with what some consider "good" movies, such as *Chariots of Fire*, *Tender Mercies*, and *A Cry in the Dark*. A noted film critic writes, "Even these sympathetic portrayals failed to show organized faith as relevant in any way to the lives of ordinary Americans" (Michael Medved, *Reader's Digest,* July 1990).

One noted writer said, "Let me give you an example of one of the finest shows on television right now: *L. A. Law.* Love that show. Excellent writing. But on that show people routinely ... sleep together if they're at all attracted to each other. ... Do you think that doesn't have anything to do with any 15-year-old hopping into the sack and getting pregnant? Do you think there is no one paying the price for the story that's being told?" (From a transcription, *My Lies Are Your Future,* broadcast by University Station WXXI).

Proud parents watched their beautiful daughter receive her academy diploma. Now their hearts ache. She moved into a rented room with a boyfriend who smokes and drinks. Where did she meet him? At the movies. "Health-care professionals are almost unanimous in citing the influence of television, rock music, videos, and movies in propelling the trend toward precocious sexuality" (*Reader's Digest,* April 1986).

Christians should want the millions of dollars they invest in Christian education to pay off. *The Fraying of America,* an essay by Robert Hughes, says: "The contest between education and TV ... has been won by TV, a medium now more debased in America than ever before. ... Most American students don't read much. ... The moronic national baby-sitter, the TV set, took care of that" (*Time,* February 3, 1992).

Amazing—the same article adds: "Statistically, most authors are dead, but some continue to speak to us with a vividness and urgency that few of the living can rival." Compare the work of a writer who died in 1915 with a current movie critic.

Dead Author: "Among the most dangerous resorts for pleasure is the theater. Instead of being a school for morality and virtue, as is so often claimed, it is the very hotbed of immorality. ... The only safe course is to shun the theater" (Ellen G. White, *The Adventist Home,* 516).

Movie Critic: "Surveys show that 32 percent of the American people don't even go out to a single movie in a year. Make no mistake: it is surely not just the high ticket prices or the gum on the seats or the easy availability of television and video tapes that keeps patrons away from the theaters. Americans are giving up on contemporary movies because they see their own deepest values so rarely reflected—or even respected—on screen" (Michael Medved, "Does Hollywood Hate Religion?" (*Reader's Digest,* July 1990).

Christians need to stand with the 32 percent who don't attend movies. It's Hollywood or heaven, not both. Here's the title and subheading of a feature article: "Trash TV, The industry's shock artists are all over the dial. They're lurid and they're loud and their credo is: anything goes as long as it gets an audience" (*Newsweek,* November 14, 1988).

Another article asks, "Is TV Ruining Our Children?" (*Time,* October 15, 1990). "Q. What is it about television that you find objectionable? A. Specifically, the excessive, gratuitous sex, violence, profanity" ("Bringing Satan to Heel," *Time,* June 19, 1989). Talking about her children on Larry King Live in October 2002, Madonna said, "They don't watch TV." Asked "why?" she stated, there's "a lot of junk on TV." If a woman who has made millions producing garbage doesn't want her children to watch TV, it's time for Christians to wise up.

In "Trained to Kill" (*Christianity Today,* August 10, 1998), David Grossman quotes the head of the American Academy of Pediatrics Task Force on Juvenile Violence saying, "Children don't naturally kill. ... They learn it from abuse and violence in the home and, most pervasively, from violence as entertainment in television, the movies, and interactive video games."

Moses threw down the tables of stone when he saw God's people dancing around the golden calf. God didn't revise the 10 commandments because the majority failed to obey them. He called Moses back to the mountain and wrote the same thing all over again.

Paul speaks to Christians who are tempted to lift the movie ban: "Beware lest anyone cheat you through philosophy and empty deceit, according to the tradition of men, according to the basic principles of the world, and not according to Christ" (Colossians 2:8).

WARNING: Movies, videos, DVD and TV may cause spiritual cataracts—vision blurs, the fine line between right and wrong is no longer sharp, you become near-sighted focusing on your own wants, but forgetting the needs of others. At last—you are blind.

When we get the first glimpse of Jesus coming in the clouds of heaven, there will be no regret for all the movies we've missed. Pray every day, "Turn away my eyes from looking at worthless things, and revive me in Your way" (Psalm 119:37).

"His way" is a *ladder* that reaches from earth to heaven. *Piety* means that in our humanity, we link with His divinity. Moses looked to Jesus and turned away from sinful pleasures. Today the sins of Egypt reach our homes via TV, Videos, DVD, and the World Wide Web. To avoid going to the wrong place on the Internet, the Christian will be quick to use the delete key.

In an article titled, "From Prime Time to Our Time" (*Reader's Digest*, August 2000), author Katherine Gibson says, "We turned off the TV and got our lives back." Let's give our time to Jesus. By resisting Hollywood entertainment, you will be stronger to resist other worldly attractions which many youth place on their list of questionable activities or practices and many other things the devil will come up with that are not on the list.

This is no time to complain, "The rules are too strict. Can't have any fun! It's a boring life." Ever since I ran away from home at 11 because I didn't like the work or the rules, I've thanked God for loving parents who took me back. I learned that the greatest joy comes from living to please my parents and my God. It's true, "The world is passing away, and the lust of it; but he who does the will of God abides forever" (1 John 2:17).

David recognized Jesus as the way when He wrote, "You will show me the path of life; In your presence is fullness of joy; at Your right hand are pleasures forevermore" (Psalm 16:11). We've never owned a TV. I've never attended a theater. Don't get me wrong. I've made my share of mistakes and disappointed Jesus many times. I've discovered, though, that my greatest joy comes when I'm doing His will.

My recreation and amusement has been in God's great outdoors. Last year my wife and I climbed Half Dome in Yosemite National Park. We chased away a mother bear and her cubs when they tried to come into our tent at 2:00 a.m. Our entire family has hiked all 220 miles on the John Muir Trail from Yosemite Valley to the top of Mount Whitney. I've had the excitement of kayaking 15 days down the longest tributary of the Amazon. Many of our happiest vacations involved backpacking. We walk every day, and God always puts something new in our path.

Moses could have been a mummy. Praise God, he's in heaven. I want to meet him. And after God brings the Holy City back to this world, I'd even welcome a chance to take a walk with Moses and Jesus. Refusing to love the things of this world, and live a life of *piety* is no sacrifice. Instead of being turned to ashes with the wicked, we'll be able to explore the universe. Instead of becoming a mummy in a museum, we can live with Jesus for eternity. Are you ready?

Keep on climbing! Cling to Jesus. "He is able to keep you from falling."

I'll forsake all worldly pleasure,
God gives PIETY.

Points to Remember
1. Moses forsook the pleasures of the world.
2. He valued a home in heaven more than anything the world offers.
3. He's an example of those who will be raised from the dead when Jesus comes.
4. Jesus is the standard. *Piety* means being like Him.
5. True Christians will completely separate from all worldly practices.
6. Jesus is the true source of joy.

Climb Higher

God Offers Piety

"Climb higher than the standard set by the world; follow where Jesus has led the way. ... By beholding Christ, by seeking Him in faith and prayer, you may become like Him" (*Counsels to Teachers*, 402).

"Faith, virtue, science, temperance, patience, *piety*, ... [are rounds] of the *ladder*. We are saved by climbing round after round, mounting step after step, to the height of Christ's ideal for us" (Translated from *Los Hechos de los Apostoles*, 422. Compare with *The Acts of the Apostles*, 530).

The Ladder

"**Will you climb the *ladder*?** Jesus Christ is our pattern, the great standard of moral character. Will you follow His example, or will you choose to follow the example and practice and customs of the world?" (*Bible Echo*, November 19, 1894).

"**You will never reach a higher standard** than you yourself set. Then set your mark high, and step by step, even though it be by painful effort, by self-denial and sacrifice, ascend the whole length of the *ladder*" (*Messages to Young People*, 99).

"**God wants you to be like Himself**. He wants to keep you unspotted from the world, to forgive your sins, and to draw you to Himself, that you may step off the *ladder* into the everlasting kingdom of our Lord and Saviour Jesus Christ" (*Review and Herald*, April 30, 1901).

"**We must keep the eye directed upward to God** above the *ladder*. The question with men and women gazing heavenward is, 'How can I obtain the mansions for the blessed?' It is by being a partaker of the divine nature. It is by escaping the 'corruption that is in the world through lust.' It is by entering into the holiest by the blood of Jesus, laying hold of the hope set before you in the gospel. It is by fastening yourself to Christ and straining every nerve to leave the world behind. ... It is ... holding on to Christ and constantly mounting upward toward God" (*Our High Calling*, 75).

Piety

"Set your mind on things above, not on things on the earth" (Colossians 3:2).

"**The religion of Jesus** is endangered. It is being mingled with worldliness. Worldly policy is taking the place of the true *piety*" (*Counsels to Writers and Editors*, 95).

"**Real *piety*** begins when all compromise with sin is at an end" (*Thoughts From the Mount of Blessing*, 91).

"**The standard of *piety*** is low among professed Christians generally, and it is hard for the young to resist the worldly influences that are encouraged by many church-members. The majority of nominal Christians, while they profess to be living for Christ, are really living for the world" (*Messages to Young People*, 374).

Live to Please God and Honor Jesus in All Things

"Let your conduct be worthy of the gospel of Christ" (Philippians 1:27).

"**The only safe course** is to shun the theater, the circus, and every other questionable amusement" (*Messages to Young People*, 380).

"**Recreation** in the open air, the contemplation of the works of God in nature, will be of the highest benefit" (*Messages to Young People*, 381).

"**Let us never lose sight** of the fact that *Jesus is a wellspring of joy.* ... If they can take Jesus with them, and maintain a prayerful spirit, they are perfectly safe" (*Messages to Young People*, 38).

Honor Jesus With Your Dress

"Put on Christ" (Galatians 3:27).

"**To dress plainly**, abstaining from display of jewelry and ornaments of every kind is in keeping with our faith" (*Testimonies for the Church*, 3:366).

"**Our clothing, while modest and simple, should be of good quality**, of becoming colors, and suited for service. It should be chosen for durability rather than display. ... Instead of struggling to meet the demands of fashion, have the courage to dress healthfully and simply" (*The Ministry of Healing*, 228, 294).

"**We are not to feel it our duty** to wear a pilgrim's dress of just such a color, just such a shape, but neat, modest apparel, that the word of inspiration teaches us we should wear. If our hearts are united with Christ's heart, we shall have a most intense desire to be clothed with His righteousness. Nothing will be put upon the person to attract attention or to create controversy" (*Testimonies to Ministers*, 130, 131).

The Standard

"*I am the way*" (John 14:6).

"**There is no higher standard** than the life of Christ" (*Medical Ministry*, 160).

"**The world rejected Christ** because his life was in such marked contrast to their own. In every generation, those who are seeking to follow His example will be distinct from the world" (*The Signs of the Times*, May 26, 1881).

"**The condition** of being received into the Lord's family is coming out from the world, separating from all its contaminating influences. ... We are to be distinguished from the world. ... As believers in the truth we are to be distinct in practice from sin and sinners. Our citizenship is in heaven" (*Fundamentals of Christian Education*, 481).

Piety Brings Joy
"These things I have spoken to you, that My joy may remain in you, and that your joy may be full" (John 15:11).

Chapter 8
Too Young?

Jesus proclaims, "I am the WAY, the truth and the life. No one comes to the Father except through me."
—John 14:6

**We are saved by climbing with Jesus.
Steps up the *ladder* include faith, science,
temperance, patience, piety, and FRATERNITY.**

ineteen-year-old Terry Nennich majored in agriculture and business management at the University of Minnesota. Before completing his first year, friends invited him to join Farmhouse Fraternity, where the Bible served as the official house book. Here he found a brotherhood of 40 men dedicated to Christian values, and who were willing to die for one another. They were loyal to the high standards of the group.

Terry thought, *This is sure different from all the fussing and bickering I used to see back in my home church.* Impressed by the love men in his fraternity showed for each other, he decided to go to Andrews University and study for the ministry. *My goal,* he thought, *will be to help people love each other the way Jesus loves us.* Today, as a church pastor, Terry faces the challenge of helping members find the joy of loving one another.

The next to the last step on the *ladder* to heaven is *fraternity. Webster's Ninth New Collegiate Dictionary* refers to *fraternity* as "a group of people associated or formally organized for a common purpose." More than this, it is "the quality or state of being brothers." It comes from the Latin *fraternus* or the French *frater* meaning brother, friendly, brotherly, and brotherhood.

Those who climb the *ladder* in preparation to live with Jesus for all of eternity will want to be all of this and more. We are to love one another. We are to show brotherly kindness. We are to prefer others above ourselves and be united in a *fraternity* with one purpose and goal—to give the gospel to all the world.

Christ's *fraternity* is His special last-day church, "who keep the commandments of God and have the testimony of Jesus Christ" (Revelation 12:17). The church is the only society in the world that is organized to benefit those who are not members. By contrast, when you join a club and pay dues, you join for the benefits you receive.

Christ's church, His *fraternity*, is organized for service. Its leader, and our Brother, Jesus, gives us an example. He declares, "Even the Son of Man did not come to be served, but to serve, and to give His life a ransom for many" (Mark 10:45).

Everyone who professes the name of Jesus faces the question, "Am I ready to give my life to save another?" How can I know that I'm truly a brother of Jesus and part of His *fraternity?* He gives us the answer. "Whoever does the will of My Father in heaven is my brother and sister" (Matthew 12:50).

Each step up the *ladder* reveals more of the will of the Father for us. We have *faith* in Jesus. We live lives of *virtue*. The *science* of the cross leads us to let Jesus cleanse us of all sin. Because our body is the temple of the Holy Spirit, we practice *temperance* to honor our Creator. We pray for *patience. Piety* and a desire to be like Jesus lead us to forsake the things of this world. But there is more.

Christ's great commission is so important, it is repeated. First, after His resurrection, Jesus talked with His disciples as they sat at the table. He challenged, "Go into all the world and preach the gospel to every creature" (Mark 16:15).

Then again, on a mountain in Galilee, Jesus declares: "All authority has been given to Me in heaven and on earth" (Matthew 28:18). Based on His universal authority, Christ commands: "Go therefore and make disciples of all the nations, baptizing them in the name of the Father and of the Son and of the Holy Spirit, teaching them to observe all things that I have commanded you; and lo, I am with you always, even to the end of the [world]" (Matthew 28:19, 20).

The command is for all who choose to climb with Jesus. It's for all who belong to His *fraternity*. As brothers and sisters of Christ we are to GO!

Sharing our faith with others has always been God's plan. Only 12 chapters into the Bible, we find God speaking to Abraham, "Leave your country, your relatives, and your father's house, and go to the land that I will show you" (Genesis 12:1, NLT).

We serve a missionary God. He told Abraham to go. He added: "In you all the families of the earth shall be blessed" (Genesis 12:3). Not just the chosen race, but the whole human race is to be blessed through Abraham's seed which is Christ.

"God had only one Son, and He was a missionary." These words written by David Livingston, pioneer missionary to Africa, are true. The Christ who left heaven and came to planet earth is the greatest missionary of all. Before His birth, the angel instructed, "You shall call His name Jesus, for He will save His people from their sins" (Matthew 1:21).

Because of His mission to save a lost world, Jesus announced early in His ministry that "Many will come from the east and west, and sit down with Abraham, Isaac, and Jacob in the kingdom of heaven" (Matthew 8:11).

Jesus served as heaven's missionary to planet earth. He calls us to follow in His footsteps. "As the Father has sent Me, I also send you" (John 20:21).

The Holy Spirit is a missionary Spirit. In His last recorded words before ascending to heaven, Jesus promised: "You shall receive power when the Holy Spirit has come upon you; and you shall be witnesses to Me in Jerusalem, and in all Judea and Samaria, and to the end of the earth" (Acts 1:8).

Home is our number one mission field. The work of proclaiming the gospel was to begin in Jerusalem—home. Jesus asks us to share heaven's love with our families, neighbors, and the people in our community. Next we are to go to our state, and then to our nation. And because we love others as much as ourselves, we go to the end of the earth to witness for our Savior. It's a global mission.

The whole Bible is a missionary book. It tells us how to live to please Jesus. It shows us how to repent and find forgiveness and salvation. It inspires us to share our faith with others. Finally, it promises success for those who join the missionary *fraternity* of Christ. John writes, "I looked, and behold, a great multitude which no one could number, of all nations, tribes, peoples, and tongues, standing before the throne and before the Lamb" (Revelation 7:9).

Those who unite in Christ's *fraternity* will soon be able to stand on the sea of glass with the saved of all ages. God's promise to Abraham 4,000 years ago will be fulfilled. Sons and daughters of God will be like the stars in the sky. Their numbers will be like the grains of sand on all the beaches of the world. "Those who are wise shall shine like the brightness of the firmament, and those who turn many to righteousness like the stars forever and ever" (Daniel 12:3).

The call to witness is for teachers, pastors, physicians, nurses, computer experts, office workers, farmers, craftsman, pilots, and every other profession. Whether we are educators, healthcare workers, ministers or evangelists, builders, manufacturers, financiers, musicians, housewives, publishers, writers, sales persons, we all have one special task. We are to join with Jesus in giving the gospel to the world.

Do you remember Jeremiah? He records his experience in the following words: "The Lord said to me: Do not say, 'I am a youth,' for you shall go to all to whom I send you" (Jeremiah 1:7). Where does God want you or me to go? He has a plan for every life, and He promises: "The Lord will guide you continually" (Isaiah 58:11).

Every person faces the question, "What will be my life-work?" Whatever occupation we choose, our chief task is witnessing for Christ. This is our most important work. God has led me every step of the way, and He's ready to lead you. I've discovered five ways to know God's will. You will find these helpful as you ask God what He wants you to do with your life.

1. Search for God's will as revealed in His Word.
2. Watch for the indications of providence.
3. Pray that the Holy Spirit will impress you.
4. Improve every opportunity by doing your best.
5. Commit yourself totally to God and His service.

I still remember sitting on a log watching moonlight flood the granite face of old Wawona Dome. It had been just a few months after I'd decided to run away from home. My loving parents had welcomed me home, and they offered to let me go to summer camp if I earned the money. I soon found jobs working for neighbors and stopped complaining about work at home.

Warmed by the blazing campfire, other boys my age sat on logs around me. Missionary Eric B. Hare grabbed our attention with tales of the haunted pagoda—how pagan devil worshipers in the jungles of Burma responded to the gospel. He saved his best for the last night. The fire burned until only embers remained, Pastor Hare spoke softly. "God is calling you boys. He wants you to be missionaries. He wants you to go to the ends of the world and tell people about Jesus. He wants you to be *fishers of men*."

That campfire changed my life—well, it wasn't really the campfire. In fact, it wasn't even Pastor Hare, though he was God's instrument. It was Jesus that changed my life that night. How could I resist His call? "Follow Me, and I will make you fishers of men" (Matthew 4:19). Led by the Holy Spirit, I determined, *I've got to become a missionary.*

Back home I read stories about amazing pioneer missionaries like Leo B. Halliwell and his medical launch ministry on the Amazon. I read about F. A. Stahl's work for Indians around Lake Titicaca. I began dreaming and praying, "Lord, if it's your will, send me to South America."

Convicted at camp that God wanted me to become a missionary, an overwhelming idea filled my mind. *You must prepare for the ministry.* I couldn't get rid of the thought. On turning 13 and newly baptized, God opened doors to fulfill my dream by sending me to a Christian high school where I lived with the principal.

To pay tuition, I did janitorial work, which meant sweeping and dusting the entire school, including the chapel. Many times after finishing my cleaning, I took my Bible and went to the front of the empty chapel. I pretended to preach God's Word to eager listeners, when in fact no one was around. Incredible shyness kept me from speaking for real in public.

Two years later at another academy, I filled out a form that asked what I wanted to do for my life's work. Of course, I wrote that I wanted to be a minister. To help overcome my shyness, I signed up for speech class, in addition to Bible, woodwork, music, and other courses.

My advisor, Mr. Wilkinson, whom I also lived with, reviewed my registration card and scowled. "You don't want to take these classes!" He tore up the card and threw the pieces to the floor. *What's going on?* I wondered. Resentful, I reached down to pick up the pieces.

Mr. Wilkinson took a new card and wrote his own course schedule for me: Bible, English, Spanish, Physics, and Geometry. I wanted to argue, but again I was much too bashful to confront a professor. *He won't even let me take speech!* I fumed. *How am I ever going to become a minister?* (But as I found out later, this would be another act of providence.)

Before the end of the first semester, the principal called me to his office to discuss my plans for the future. "Our records show you want to become a minister. We've been watching. You are too shy to ever be a pastor."

Though I remained respectful, I thought, *Who are you to tell me what I should do? I've been asking God to guide me!* He went on to tell me that my teachers thought I should study medicine based on my excellent work in science and math.

"But Sir," I finally got up courage to speak. "I want to become a missionary more than anything else!"

"All right," he smiled. "You can be a missionary doctor."

I left his office discouraged and with a new dilemma I hadn't expected. *Should I become a doctor or a minister?* I felt strongly that the Lord wanted me to be a minister, and I knew that only He could lead me out of this apparent roadblock.

During the next semester, my Bible class teacher asked me to research and write a paper on literature evangelism. I soon discovered that an inspired Christian writer, Ellen G. White, considered literature evangelism—selling Christian books—to be "the very best preparation for the ministry." This intrigued me!

Just days later at a chapel service, some Christian publishing men were asking students to spend the summer selling books. It sounded perfect for me, so I overcame my shyness enough to pull myself out of the seat and walk to the front of the chapel. I listened excitedly as I heard students making plans to enter into *the very best preparation for the ministry.*

When they got to me, one leader asked, "How old are you, son?" When I told him, he said, "I'm sorry, we won't be able to use you. You're too young."

Too young? My heart sank into my shoes, and I turned to walk away. I'd been praying so hard that if God wanted me to be a minister, He would help me sell books. If I didn't sell any, I'd study medicine. But now they wouldn't even give me a chance.

But back in my room, I felt compelled to write a letter to another Christian publishing representative. Amazingly, a few days later, I got a phone call from him. "I'll meet you at your school at 1:30 Thursday afternoon," he said. I spoke in my lowest voice so he wouldn't think I was too young. *But what's he going to say when he sees me?* I wondered.

Whatever he thought about my appearance, he agreed to let me spend the next summer selling books in my hometown. He even promised to send someone to train me to be successful. Determined to know God's will for my life, every day after school I went to my closet and prayed. "Lord, if you want me to become a minister, please help me sell books. If I don't sell any, I'll know you want me to become a doctor."

I wasn't given much of a chance. I wrote to my parents and told them about my plans for the summer, but mother wrote back, "You never could sell anything, but if that's what you want to do, it's all right."

And by the time my trainer, Adam, left after working with me for a day and a half, he said, "If you don't do anything else this summer, pray, pray, pray!" Noticing just how bashful I was, he never actually asked me to even practice a sales presentation in front of him!

My teachers and parents were right about questioning my ability for the job. In fact, when I gave my first pitch for the books, they jumped around in my hands because I shook so much. My mother was right—I couldn't sell anything.

But the Lord knows how to sell books. He sold that first set of books in the very first home I made a presentation! So from 1:00 to 9:00 every day for four months, God kept impressing people to buy books—lots of books. I also learned that Mr. Wilkinson's rewrite of my schedule at the start of the school year had actually enabled me to have nearly enough courses to enter college, where even greater preparation for ministry was possible. I quickly signed up for two correspondence courses, one being advanced Spanish, and by the end of summer, I had enough credits to enter college.

In addition, the Lord had sold so many books for me that I earned a full scholarship. He had answered my prayers, and I knew He wanted me to be His minister. Thankful, I enrolled in a ministerial course at Pacific Union College in Northern California. I graduated, and the Lord gave me a call to full-time ministry.

Last, yet God's very best gift—marriage to a lovely young nurse who said she would go anywhere in the world with me. We took our honeymoon in Mexico, and after we returned, sent our names to the mission board at our church's world headquarters.

For sometime, no call came for us. We even spoke with church leaders who said, "We don't need North American pastors to serve outside the country. If you were a teacher or a doctor, sure, but not a pastor." They suggested we keep working in America, and even more, to buy a house.

We began praying, "Lord, if you really want us to be missionaries, please give us a call before we buy a home that will tie us up financially." Soon we were given a call to build a new church and conduct evangelistic meetings. It looked like we were going to be there for a long time. So as advised, we began house hunting.

It wasn't long until we found an affordable house and began looking to borrow money for a down payment. One evening, at a motel, my wife and I had a very serious talk with the Lord. "Loving Father, You know we are willing to serve You as overseas missionaries. No doors have opened. We ask that Your will be done."

Early the next morning, the phone rang. "Your loan has been approved. You can close your deal on the house when the bank opens at 10:00." That was a mere two hours away. It seemed the Lord had answered our prayer—and indeed He had. But He ended up surprising us.

An hour later, the phone rang again. But this time, it was a church administrator. "We just received a call for you to serve in the Lake Titicaca Mission in the Andes of Peru."

What's gong on? I wondered. I didn't think they needed any pastors serving as missionaries! The leader continued, "We don't want you to accept this call. We need you here."

I had to be honest and replied, "We've prayed for months that if God wanted us to serve as foreign missionaries, He would give us a call before we buy a house. If you had called just an hour later, we would have been closing the deal on a new home. God must want us to go."

The next morning, we officially accepted the call. We were asked to be ready to leave in 30 days. However, one month later, we learned that getting a permit from the Peruvian government to work in that country was proving difficult. Months—*months!*—began to pass, and still no permit.

While waiting for the go ahead to Peru, I joined a group of volunteers to tear down a building on property donated for a new church welfare center. While someone went to get a ladder so we could tear off the roof, others began knocking off siding. As more and more volunteers arrived, I went inside to knock off the last of the siding.

Before I knew it, the building started to give way. I literally dove for the door, but I didn't make it. Believing it was the end, I prayed as the building came down. I was crushed under a gabled roof that fell flat, but terrible pain told me I was still alive. "Thank you, Lord," I prayed.

I was soon rescued, but the injuries were severe. It took 21 stitches to sew my right ear back in place, and X-rays revealed four broken ribs and a right leg that was broken in seven places. In surgery, it took three screws to put my leg back in order, and an orthopedist said, "You have the worst possible fractures. It will be at least a year before you can walk again."

A year? Just two days later, word came that our permit for Peru had been approved.

Friends visiting me at the hospital said, "Now you know the Lord doesn't want you to go to Peru." But I wasn't buying it— not after all the Lord had done. He gave me the courage to reply, "It's the devil who doesn't want me to go."

Three months later, the orthopedist came out holding up x-rays. "It's a miracle," he exclaimed. "We'll give the Great Physician credit for this." Though for several months I'd need to use crutches and later a cane, God had worked a miracle on my leg. Eventually, I would walk without any aid at all!

Exactly one week after my cast was removed, my wife and I were on a plane flying to Peru, thankful that a God who says, "Go," makes it possible despite all of the devil attempts to thwart Him. When we arrived, we were told, "We've sent missionaries home like this, but you're the first one to arrive on crutches." To this day, I have a cane as a souvenir of what God can do for those willing to go. Before long, my wife and I walked over 100 miles to visit the Tambopata mission station in the Lake Titicaca Mission. It's true, everyone in God's *fraternity* will be plagued by an enemy who wants to discourage us from doing God's will. We must cling to Jesus and never give up. We must never let anything keep us from taking the gospel to the world.

I believe my Christian school principal was right when he said, "You're too shy to become a minister," and the publishing men knew what they were talking about when they said, "You're too young." Even my Mom told the truth when she wrote, "You never could sell anything." The leader from my church's world headquarters understood the importance of using nationals to give the gospel when he said, "We don't need North American pastors to serve overseas." My orthopedist knew how long it would take for bones to heal when he said, "you won't be able to walk for a year."

But best of all, God is more right when He calls us to be part of His worldwide *fraternity*. He gives us an impossible assignment, and then makes it possible. I'll always thank Him for sending a man who spent hours driving to my school to give a bashful boy a chance. No one is too young to share the faith.

The gospel will go to all the world. You can reach the top of the *ladder!* And my friend, whether you're 18 or 81, God has a plan for your life. Jesus calls us to be part of His worldwide *fraternity*. He prayed, That they all may be *one*, as You, Father, are in Me, and I in You; that they also may be one in Us, that the world may believe that You sent Me" (John 17:21).

We are to be "looking for and hastening the coming of the day of God" (2 Peter 3:12). Jesus promised, "And this gospel of the kingdom will be preached in all the world as a witness to all the nations, and then the end will come" (Matthew 24:14). More than anything else, He wants you to share Jesus' love with family, friends, and the world. Climbing the *ladder* with Jesus means finding others and helping them climb the *ladder* too.

I will share my faith with others,
God's FRATERNITY

Points to Remember
1. Jesus invites you to join His *fraternity*.
2. His *fraternity*, the church, exists to give the gospel to the world.
3. Sharing the faith is everybody's business.
4. Find God's will for your life by total commitment to His service.
5. Ask Jesus to help you stay strong when Satan places difficulties in your way.
6. Watch for God to open doors of opportunity.
7. Jesus will guide you continually.

Climb Higher

God Offers Fraternity
Success in the Christian warfare means ... constant, earnest striving for higher and still higher attainments in the Christian life. It means helping others to climb heavenward" (*Manuscript Releases*, 20:30).

"Faith, virtue, science, temperance, patience, piety, *fraternity* ... [are rounds] of the *ladder*. We are saved by climbing round after round, mounting step after step, to the height of Christ's ideal for us" (Translated from *Los Hechos de los Apostoles*, 422. Compare with *The Acts of the Apostles*, 530).

The Ladder

"Only by Christ's aid can we be saved. ... We can reach heaven only by the mystic *ladder* Jesus Christ; and He came to this earth that we might be enabled to do this" (*The Signs of the Times*, January 6, 1898).

"There are not many ways to heaven. Each one may not choose his own way. Christ says, 'I am the way. ... He was the way when Adam lived, when Abel presented to God the blood of the slain lamb, representing the blood of the Redeemer. Christ was the way by which patriarchs and prophets were saved. He is the way by which alone we can have access to God" (*The Desire of Ages*, 663).

Fraternity

"Be of one mind, having compassion for one another; *love [fraternally]*" (1 Peter 3:8).

"That which we have seen and heard we declare to you, that you also may have fellowship with us; and truly our fellowship is with the Father and with His Son Jesus Christ" (1 John 1:3).

"I believe in *Fraternity*, that mystic virtue that binds me to every man and makes me to hear the cry of his blood wherever it is wasted, whether at my doorstep or in the uttermost parts of the earth" (Arna Bontemps, *The Napa Register*, September 22, 1981).

"Each nationality should labor earnestly for every other nationality. There is but one Lord, one faith. Our effort should be to answer Christ's prayer for His disciples, that they should be one. ... We are to demonstrate to the world that men of every nationality are one in Christ Jesus" (*Testimonies for the Church*, 9:195, 196).

God's Fraternity Called Out

"Come out of her, my people, lest you share in her sins" (Revelation 18:4).

"And the dragon was wroth with the woman, and went to make war with the *remnant* of her seed, which *keep the com-*

mandments of God and *have the testimony of Jesus Christ*"
(Revelation 12:17).

"The testimony of Jesus is the spirit of prophecy"
(Revelation 19:10)."Repent and be baptized in the name of
Jesus Christ for the remission of sins; and you shall receive the
gift of the Holy Spirit. ... Then those who gladly received his
word were baptized; ... and the Lord added to the church daily
those who were being saved" (Acts 2:38, 41, 47).

The Global Mission of Christ's Fraternity

"This gospel of the kingdom will be preached in all the
world" (Matthew 24:14).

"**Go to the farthest part of the habitable globe** [He bade
them] and be assured that My presence will be with you even
there. Labor in faith and confidence; for the time will never
come when I will forsake you. I will be with you always, helping you to perform your duty, guiding, comforting, sanctify-
ing, sustaining you, giving you success in speaking words that
shall draw the attention of others to heaven"
(*The Acts of the Apostles*, 29).

"**The church of Christ** is God's appointed agency for the
salvation of men. Its mission is to carry the gospel to the
world. And the obligation rests upon all Christians" (*Steps to
Christ*, 81).

"**With such an army of workers as our youth**, rightly
trained, might furnish, how soon the message of a crucified,
risen, and soon-coming Saviour might be carried to the whole
world!" (*Messages to Young People*, 196).

Life Work for Members of Christ's Fraternity

"Those who are wise ... turn many to righteousness"
(Daniel 12:3).

"**The work above all work** . . . is the work of saving souls
for whom Christ has died. Make this the main, the important
work of your life. Make it your special life work" (*Messages to
Young People*, 227).

"**God calls for those of all classes and all trades** to work in His cause. Those are wanted who will begin at the lower rounds of the *ladder*. ... Let diligent, persevering effort be put forth for others, with earnest prayer for the aid of divine grace and power, and great results will follow missionary labor" (*Life Sketches of Ellen G. White*, 274).

"**The very best talent** that can be secured is needed to educate and mold the minds of the young, and to carry on successfully the many lines of work that will need to be done by the teacher in our church schools" (*Messages to Young People*, 221).

Rules to Guide in Choice of Occupation

"**To do our best** in the work that lies nearest, to commit our ways to God, and to watch for the indications of His providence—these are rules that ensure safe guidance in the choice of an occupation" (*Education*, 267).

"**God gives opportunities;** success depends upon the use made of them. The openings of Providence must be quickly discerned and eagerly entered" (*Messages to Young People*, 148).

"**Those who decide** to do nothing in any line that will displease God, will know, after presenting their case before Him, just what course to pursue" (*The Desire of Ages*, 668).

Chapter 9
Know How to Love

Jesus proclaims, "I am the WAY, the truth and the life.
No one comes to the Father except through me."
—John 14:6

We are saved by climbing with Jesus.
Steps up the *ladder* include faith, science,
temperance, patience, piety, fraternity, and LOVE.

*M*ark's rebellion began with little things, such as stealing cookies from a cookie jar. When Christian parents showed *love* in trying to get him to shape up and obey, he exploded, "No one is going to tell me what to do! I want to be free!"

Soon, petty theft and robbery led to skirmishes with the police. As a teenager, he joined a gang. At the beginning, it was only a little meanness. Then one night his gang decided to have additional excitement. "Let's go to a neighboring town and hold up the druggist," one young man suggested. "Let's have a real thrill!"

"That's cool," Mark agreed. "We'll have the thrill of holding up a man. He won't put up a fight. There won't be any trouble."

These young men didn't reckon properly. The old man did put up a fight, and during the holdup he was shot. In the courtroom scene that followed, they all pointed the finger at Mark. He held the gun. He pulled the trigger. The judge sentenced him to die in the electric chair.

Everyone did all they could. Friends tried to come to his rescue. His parents went to the governor. "Please change our son's sentence to life in prison instead of death," they pleaded.

"I know how you feel," the judge responded, "but the evidence is clear. The case must stand. The sentence must remain."

While Mark was in his cell waiting execution, Christian youth came and sang, read their Bibles, prayed, and went on their way—all without effect. Then one day, Jeremy, a member of a prison ministry team, noticed Mark and saw his great need.

"Mark, let's talk," he suggested. At first the young prisoner didn't want to listen, but Jeremy didn't give up. Each time he came, he tried to be a friend. Finally after many visits, he convinced Mark that God loves young men even on death row. Jesus died to save murderers too.

Divine *love* broke through Mark's hard heart. He knelt and prayed, pouring out his heart to a forgiving God. "Give me faith to *love* and serve You. Please forgive me for the terrible sins I've committed. Forgive me for killing a man." Right there in his death cell, not long before he would walk down the "last mile of the way," as it was known, he accepted by faith the amazing *love* of a wonderful Savior.

Jeremy taught Mark the song, "No One Ever Cared for Me Like Jesus." He often sang it, and it had a very important effect on his fellow prisoners.

When the day of death arrived, everyone said, "He'll break. He hasn't yet, he's kept up a good front, but he'll break—they all do. Just wait till he looks down the corridor and sees the little green door—he'll break down."

At last, Mark and the chaplain, a guard on either side, and reporters who came to record the sad story started down the corridor and made the turn facing death's room.

Mark paused. Everyone watched intently. *What's he going to do, what will he say?* they wondered. After just a moment, the young man threw out his chest, a smile broke out over his face, and he began to sing:

"I would *love* to tell you what I think of Jesus
    Since I found in Him a friend so strong and true;

I would tell you how He changed my life completely,
He did something that no other friend could do.

"No one ever cared for me like Jesus,
There's no other friend so kind as He;
No one else could take the sin and darkness from me,
O how much He cared for me."

With firm steady steps, Mark kept walking slowly past barred cells. In these cages, men waited for their day when they too would march down this row. They were grasping the bars with all their might till their knuckles turned white as they witnessed the face of a young man who was able to sing going to his death.

How could he do it? Down those hard faces, tears rolled freely. And down the faces of reporters, men who were accustomed to the hard, the morbid, the bitter things of life—they too felt the trickle of tears down their faces. Never had they witnessed a sight like this.

Mark kept on walking—right on through the little green door—still singing as he sat down in the electric chair:

"Ev'ry day He comes to me with new assurance,
More and more I understand His words of *love*;
But I'll never know just why He came to save me,
'Til some day I see His blessed face above."
—C. F. Weigle

Folks said, "Soon the current will strike and life will be gone. It will be the end. He may have hope of some sort—something's holding him up, but it will soon be over. It will be for naught. It won't do him any good."

Mark knew better. He had learned to *love* a Jesus who is soon to come. He knew his waiting time would be only a little while. As far as he was concerned, the next moment, he would hear the voice of Jesus calling. It wasn't the end.

Let's face it: Whether we like it or not, "The wages of sin is death" (Romans 6:23). The first time I lied to my parents, the day I stole lumber to build a raft, the time I got angry with my brother—all these things, or any one of them, and many more, put me on death row.

But praise God, this is not the end of the story! The rest of Romans 6:23 says, "The gift of God is eternal life in Christ Jesus our Lord." God loves us with perfect *love*. "God demonstrates His own *love* toward us, in that while we were still sinners, Christ died for us" (Romans 5:8). Our loving God does not want to leave us in sin. Scripture assures us, "The blood of Jesus Christ His Son cleanses us from all sin" (1 John 1:7).

God's perfect *love* provides us with assurance of everlasting life. "For God so loved the world that He gave His only begotten Son, that whoever believes in Him should not perish but have everlasting life" (John 3:16).

God in His eternal *love* gives us Jesus. He's a *ladder* to climb all the way to heaven and the very last step is *love*. Is this *His love* or *our love*? The Bible says, "We *love* Him because He first loved us" (1 John 4:19).

The final step to the kingdom is our *love* for Him. Through the power of the Holy Spirit, "Christ may dwell in your hearts through *faith* [the first step on the *ladder*]; that you, being rooted and grounded in *love* [the last step on the *ladder*], may be able to comprehend with all the saints what is the width and length and depth and height—to know the *love* of Christ which passes knowledge, that you may be filled with all the fullness of God" (Ephesians 3:17-19).

To make sure we understand, Paul admonishes: "Walk in *love* as Christ also has loved us and given Himself for us" (Ephesians 5:2). The last step before leaping off the *ladder* into heaven is our *love*, our response to God's grace and *love*.

I *love* strawberries. I *love* sailing. I *love* my wife. I *love* Jesus. We use the same word—*love*—but what are we talking about? Here are some of Webster's Collegiate Dictionary definitions of *love*: "to please, strong affection for another, benevolence, an assurance of *love*, devotion or admiration, unselfish loyal and benevolent concern for the good of another, the fatherly concern of God for humankind, brotherly concern for others, a person's adoration of God."

Now let's examine *love* from a Bible perspective. "This is *love*, that we walk according to His commandments" (2 John 6). In His reply to a Pharisee lawyer, Jesus makes it simple: "You shall *love* the Lord your God with all your heart, with all your soul, and with all your mind. This is the first and great commandment, and the second is like it: You shall *love* your neighbor as yourself. On these two commandments hang all the Law" (Matthew 22:37-40).

To help us know how to *love* God and others, Jesus wrote the following words with His own finger on two tables of stone:

Love God
1. "You shall have no other gods before Me.
2. "You shall not make for yourself a carved image, or any likeness of anything that is in heaven above, or that is in the earth beneath, or that is in the water under the earth; you shall not bow down to them nor serve them. For I, the Lord your God, am a jealous God, visiting the iniquity of the fathers on the children to the third and fourth generations of those who hate Me, but showing mercy to thousands, to those who *love* Me and keep My commandments.
3. "You shall not take the name of the Lord your God in vain, for the Lord will not hold him guiltless who takes His name in vain.
4. "Remember the Sabbath day, to keep it holy. Six days you shall labor and do all your work, but the seventh day is the Sabbath of the Lord your God. In it you shall do no work: you, nor your son, nor your daughter, nor your manservant, nor your maidservant, nor your cattle, nor your stranger who is within your gates. For in six days the Lord made the heavens and the earth, the sea, and all that is in them, and rested the seventh day.

Therefore the Lord blessed the Sabbath day and hallowed it" (Exodus 20:3-11).

Love Others

1. "Honor your father and your mother, that your days may be long upon the land which the Lord your God is giving you.
2. "You shall not murder.
3. "You shall not commit adultery.
4. "You shall not steal.
5. "You shall not bear false witness against your neighbor.
6. "You shall not covet your neighbor's house; you shall not covet your neighbor's wife, nor his manservant, nor his maidservant, nor his ox, nor his donkey, nor anything that is your neighbor's" (Exodus 20:12-17).

In talking about *love*, Jesus declared, "He who has My commandments and keeps them, it is he who loves Me" (John 14:21). Let's thank Jesus for showing us how to *love*.

Let's praise Him for giving us 10 rules to guide our footsteps as we climb toward the kingdom. Remember, "Eye has not seen, nor ear heard, nor have entered into the heart of man the things which God has prepared for those who *love* Him" (1 Corinthians 2:9).

Jesus knows that only those who *love* will reach heaven. After promising to prepare a place where we can enjoy the pleasures of eternity, He challenges us with these words: "If you *love* Me, keep My commandments" (John 14:15). The final chapter in the Bible reminds us that Jesus is coming soon. It also says, "Blessed are those who do His commandments, that they may have the right to the tree of life, and may enter through the gates into the city" (Revelation 22:14).

"Wait a minute!" you say. "Isn't this getting legalistic?" No! It's actually getting more loving.

"But aren't we saved by grace through faith?" Absolutely! Paul says, "We have received grace ... for obedience to the faith" (Romans 1:5). Later he asks, "Do we then make void the law through faith? Certainly not! On the contrary, we establish the law" (Romans 3:31). *Love* is a gift from Jesus. "The *love* of God has been poured out in our hearts by the Holy Spirit who was given to us" (Romans 5:5).

Peter walked on water. Glancing toward his companions in the boat, he must have thought, *Boy, will this impress them!* He began to sink. *Oh, no!*, he fears. *I'm going to drown!* Turning his eyes to Jesus he cries out, "Lord, save me!"

Jesus takes Peter's hand. They walk side by side with Peter's hand grasping the hand of his Savior. Together they step into the boat. Only with Jesus can we safely go toward His kingdom. Jesus shows us how to *love.*

Pharisees and Sadducees pretended to obey in order to impress people. This is legalism. Jesus invites us to obey to please Him. This is *love.* "Let all that you do be done with love" (1 Corinthians 16:14). "Love must be sincere. Hate what is evil. Cling to what is good" (Romans 12:9, NIV).

Peter fished all night without catching even one fish. Jesus came and said, "Cast the net on the right side of the boat" (John 21:6). Peter and the other disciples obeyed. Peter dragged the net to shore and counted 153 fish. Jesus' last recorded conversation with Peter (see John 21:15-17) took place at breakfast on the beach. Peter had finished eating when the Savior turned to him and asked a very personal question:

"Do you *love* Me?"

Peter doesn't claim to *love* Jesus more than anyone else. He simply responds, "You know I *love* you."

Christ asks again, "Do you *love* Me?"

Peter trusts Jesus to read His mind. He answers, "You know I *love* you."

It hits like an arrow in his heart when the Savior questions him a third time: "Do you *love* me?"

Peter's feelings are hurt. He wonders, *Why is Jesus asking me so many times?* He blurts out, "You know I *love* you!"

Each time Peter answers, Jesus gives him something to do.

"Feed my lambs. Tend My sheep. Feed my sheep."

Peter is asked to show *love* by serving others. Converted by Christ's perfect *love* and compelled by the Holy Spirit, Peter preached on the day of Pentecost. The man who denied his Savior three times learned how to *love*. With Jesus in control of his life, 3,000 were baptized in one day.

Is it easy to *love*? Peter's *love* for Jesus put him on a cross. Considering it too great an honor to die the way Jesus did, he asked to be crucified with his head down.

Do you know how to *love*? Do you *love* your parents? Do you *love* your spouse? Do you *love* your children? Do you *love* your neighbors? Do you *love* Jesus? Do you want to live to please Him? "Keep yourselves in the *love* of God, looking for the mercy of our Lord Jesus Christ unto eternal life" (Jude 21).

God will bless as you take the last step on the *ladder* to heaven. *Love!* "*Love* the Lord your God, that you may obey His voice, and that you may cling to Him, for He is your life" (Deuteronomy 30:20). "Now to Him who is able to keep you from stumbling, and to present you faultless before the presence of His glory with exceeding joy" (Jude 24).

More and more I LOVE the Savior,
Jesus died for me.

Points to Remember
1. Sin placed all of us on death row.
2. Jesus offers us the gift of eternal life.
3. His blood cleanses us from sin.
4. We show our *love* by obedience to His commandments.
5. God's grace gives power to obey.
6. God's perfect *love* is the motive for living to please Jesus.
7. Jesus is the means of salvation.
8. *Love* is the condition.
9. Obedience is the result.
10. Heaven is the reward.

Climb Higher

God Offer Love

"God ... gave His Son to die for us, that we might be sanctified through His grace ... His law is the echo of His own voice, giving to all the invitation, 'Come up higher. Be holy, holier still'" (*Signs of the Times*, May 28, 1902).

"Faith, virtue, science, temperance, patience, piety, fraternity, *love*, are the rounds of the *ladder*. We are saved by climbing round after round, mounting step after step, to the height of Christ's ideal for us" (Translated from *Los Hechos de los Apostoles*, 422. Compare with *The Acts of the Apostles*, 530).

The Ladder

"**Infinite *love*** has cast up a pathway upon which the ransomed of the Lord may pass from earth to heaven. That path is the Son of God. Angel guides are sent to direct our erring feet. Heaven's glorious *ladder* is let down in every man's path, barring his way to vice and folly" (*Our High Calling*, 11).

"**We point you to the mansions Christ is preparing** for all those who *love* Him. ... We point you to the *ladder* set up on earth, reaching to the city of God. Plant your feet on the *ladder*. Forsake your sins. Climb step by step and you will reach God above the *ladder*, and the Holy City of God" (*Our High Calling*, 75).

"**When the successive steps have all been mounted**, when the graces have been added one after another, the crowning grace is the perfect *love* of God—supreme *love* to God and *love* to our fellow men. And then the abundant entrance into the kingdom of God" (*Our High Calling*, 75).

Love

"You who love the Lord, hate evil!" (Psalm 97:10).

"**This last step in the *ladder*** gives to the will a new spring of action. ... This *love* is not something kept apart from our life, but it takes hold of the entire being. The heaven to which the Christian is climbing will be attained only by those who have this crowning grace. ... *Love* is the great controlling power. When *love* leads, all the faculties of mind and spirit are enlisted. *Love* to God and *love* to man will give the clear title to heaven" (*Our High Calling*, 73).

"**Righteousness is love**" (*Thoughts from the Mount of Blessing*, 18).

"**Love is the golden chain which binds believing hearts** to one another in willing bonds of friendship, tenderness, and faithful constancy, and which binds the soul to God" (*Testimonies for the Church*, 3:187).

God's Love

"I have loved you with an everlasting *love*" (Jeremiah 31:3).

"Behold what manner of *love* the Father has bestowed on us, that we should be called children of God!" (1 John 3:1).

"We have known and believed the *love* that God has for us. God is *love*" (1 John 4:16).

"**There is nothing so great** and so powerful as God's *love* for those who are His children" (Ellen G. White, *Review and Herald*, March 15, 1906.

Our Love

"You shall *love* the Lord your God with all your heart, with all your soul, and with all your might" (Deuteronomy 6:5).

"You shall *love* your neighbor as yourself" (Leviticus 19:18).

"**Love** is expressed in obedience" (*The Youth's Instructor*, July 26, 1894).

"**The ten commandments, Thou shalt, and Thou shalt not, are ten promises.** ... The terms of salvation for every son and daughter of Adam are here outlined. ... That law of ten precepts of the greatest *love* that can be presented to man is the voice of God from heaven speaking to the soul in promise, 'This do, and you will not come under the dominion and control of Satan.' There is not a negative in that law, although it may appear thus. It is DO and Live" (*God's Amazing Grace*, 134).

Perfect Love

"Perfect *love* casts out fear. ... He who fears has not been made perfect in *love*" (1 John 4:18).

"**True sanctification** means perfect *love*, perfect obedience, perfect conformity to the will of God. We are to be sanctified to God through obedience to the truth. ... We are not yet perfect; but it is our privilege to cut away from the entanglements of self and sin, and advance to perfection. Great possibilities, high and holy attainments, are placed within the reach of all" (*The Acts of the Apostles*, 565).

"**Christ ... came as an expression of the perfect *love* of God**, ... not to crush, not to judge and condemn, but to heal every weak, defective character, to save men and women from Satan's power" (*Medical Ministry*, 20).

Abiding in Love

"As the Father loved Me, I also have loved you; abide in My *love*. If you keep My commandments, you will abide in My *love*, just as I have kept My Father's commandments and abide in His *love*. These things I have spoken to you, that My joy may remain in you, and that your joy may be full" (John 15:9-11).

"**I entreat of you to hide in Jesus**, to be His own true child, walking in *love* and obedience to all His requirements, exemplifying in your life the character of Jesus—tender and thoughtful of others, considering them just as good and just as deserving as yourself of conveniences and comforts and happiness" (*Daughters of God*, 167).

"**When Christ dwells in the heart**, the soul will be so filled with His *love*, with the joy of communion with Him, that it will cleave to Him; and in the contemplation of Him, self will be forgotten. *Love* to Christ will be the spring of action" (*Steps to Christ*, 44, 45).

"**Those who feel the constraining *love* of God**, do not ask how little may be given to meet the requirements of God; they do not ask for the lowest standard, but aim at perfect conformity to the will of their Redeemer" (*Steps to Christ*, 44, 45).

Chapter 10
You Can Be Sure

"My foot has held fast to His steps;
I have kept His way and not turned aside."
—Job 23:11

"You ou can stay in Hotel Panama. It's on us," the lady at
the airline counter smiled. *No way,* I thought. *She
wants to save money and put us in a cheap hotel.*

"Ma'am," I pulled out our ticket folder. "Here's the letter
saying you will put us up in Hotel Roosevelt."

"That's all right sir, but you don't have to stay there."

A Panamanian taxi driver tapped me on the shoulder. "Are
you Mr. Muir? I came to take you and your wife to Hotel
Roosevelt. You'll like it."

The lady at the counter looked at me. "Sir, you don't have
to go with him. When you bought your tickets, all hotels were
full, but there have been cancellations. There's plenty of room
in Hotel Panama. I'll arrange for a taxi to take you."

"No! No!" the cab driver insisted. "Come with me."

I turned to my wife. "Let's go to Hotel Roosevelt." The airline agent gave me a strange look.

The driver helped us with our luggage and we climbed into
his rickety old taxi. After several tries, the engine started and
we were off. Anything but experienced travelers, we were on
our way to our first ever overseas mission assignment in South
America.

Only minutes from the airport, we passed a modern hotel
overlooking the Panama Canal with its famous locks. "What
hotel is that?" I asked the driver. "That's Hotel Panama," he

answered in broken English. I began wondering, *What will Hotel Roosevelt be like?*

The taxi kept going and going. We moved slowly in heavy traffic. My wife commented, "It's sure taking us a long time to get there."

Forty-five minutes after leaving the airport, we were in a poor section of the city when the cab finally turned in through an archway. "Hotel Roosevelt!" I looked at my wife. "This may have been a great hotel in its day, but it sure looks run down now."

The driver searched for someone to check us in at the front desk. We were the only guests in the hotel. Meals were included in the deal. When we went to the dining room for supper, they said, "We don't have any food. Tell us what you would like, and we'll send someone out to buy it. We asked for fruit. After over an hour, they finally served us bread and bananas.

Back in the room, it was hot, humid, and no air conditioning. Open windows had no screens. The bed felt like a rock. All night long, we turned, tossed, and fought mosquitoes. With all the heat, a cold shower didn't seem too bad, but there wasn't much water.

Still half asleep, we wandered into the dining room for breakfast. They offered us oatmeal, eggs, and toast. Then the waiter said, "I'm going out to buy it."

It took him so long, we ended up eating a couple of bananas left over from the evening before. We ran to get our luggage and catch a taxi, hoping not to miss our flight. Ten minutes from the airport, we passed this marvelous hotel. This time we could see the big sign, Panama Hilton.

We laughed, but we really wanted to cry. Because I failed to trust the airline agent, we'd just spent one of the most miserable nights in our lives. We could have stayed in the Hilton with a great view looking out over the Panama Canal. We could have had a good bed, air conditioning, hot showers. and all the food we could possibly eat.

Solomon wrote, "There is a way *that seems* right to a man, but its end is the way of death" (Proverbs 14:12). We lost a chance to spend a night in a good hotel because I chose to listen to the wrong voice. Will I lose out on living forever with Jesus by listening to Satan?

James admonishes, "Therefore submit to God. Resist the devil and he will flee from you" (James 4:7). First submit. That's the hard part. Those who plan to get to the top of the *ladder* must submit their wills completely to Jesus. That's why He taught us to pray, "Your will be done" (Matthew 6:10).

Once we have submitted all to Christ, we would rather die than sin. Jesus said, "Be faithful until death, and I will give you the crown of life" (Revelation 2:10). Don't be surprised if you find it easier to die for Christ than to live for Him. Jesus warned, "Narrow is the gate and difficult is the way that leads to life" (Matthew 7:14).

We can never reach heaven without the Savior. After promising mansions, He says, "I am the way" (John 14:6). We cannot save ourselves. We cannot get to the top of the *ladder* on our own. Salvation comes from Jesus. "There is no other name under heaven given among men by which we must be saved" (Acts 4:12).

Just like the Panamanian taxi driver made Hotel Roosevelt sound attractive, Satan is busy convincing us to choose the way of the world, the broad way. Jesus wants to take us by way of the cross, the narrow way. There are steps to climb.

Why go to a rundown motel when you can stay in the Hilton? Why die when you can have eternal life? Peter wrote, "Blessed be the God and Father of our Lord Jesus Christ, who according to His abundant mercy has begotten us again to a living hope through the resurrection of Jesus Christ from the dead, to an inheritance incorruptible and undefiled and that does not fade away, reserved in heaven for you who are kept by the power of God through *faith* for salvation" (1 Peter 1:3-5).

Jesus has a place reserved in heaven for you. It makes the Panama Hilton look like a slum. The airline tried to put us up in the best hotel in the country. I simply did not believe the airline wanted us to have the best. I lacked *faith* in the company providing our transportation.

Never forget, "We are kept by the power of God through *faith*. Peter explains that we obtain "*faith* ... by the righteousness of our God and Savior Jesus Christ" (2 Peter 1:1).

Again Peter declares, "His divine power has given to us all things that pertain to life and godliness, through the knowledge of Him who called us by glory and virtue, by which have been given to us exceedingly great and precious promises, that through these you may be partakers of the divine nature" (2 Peter 1:3, 4).

He continues: "For this very reason, giving all diligence, add to your faith virtue, to virtue science, to science temperance, to temperance patience, to patience piety, to piety fraternity, to fraternity love" (2 Peter 1:5-7, author's translation).

The steps on the *ladder* are straight out of God's Word. A fisherman who followed Jesus recorded them for us. Different Bible translations vary slightly, but they all start out with *faith*. Peter says, "Add to your *faith*." "Add" means we have something to do. We can never do what God does, and He won't do what we can do. We can never save ourselves. God does that. He doesn't form our character. That's our responsibility, but He sends the Holy Spirit to help us.

God's gift of *faith* finds fullness in *love*. It requires the total gift of self. Scripture says, "Even the demons believe" (James 2:19), but belief alone will not save the devil or anyone else.

God gave us a *ladder*, not an escalator. The first step, *faith*, and the last step, *love*, put it all together. *Faith* is not enough. There's more. Paul wrote, "Though I have all *faith*, so that I could remove mountains, but have not *love*, I am nothing" (1 Corinthians 13:2).

"For we through the Spirit eagerly wait for the hope of righteousness by *faith*. For in Christ Jesus neither circumcision nor uncircumcision avails anything, but *faith working through love*" (Galatians 5:5, 6). Righteousness by *faith* is *faith* working by *love*. It's our *love* responding to God's *love*. "And the grace of our Lord was exceedingly abundant, with *faith* and *love* which are in Christ Jesus" (1 Timothy 1:4). Climbing the *ladder* is *faith* working by *love.*

Faith and *love* tie all the steps together. We need to be "putting on the breastplate of *faith* and *love,* and as a helmet the hope of salvation" (1 Thessalonians 5:8). When we exercise *faith* by climbing the *ladder,* Jesus fills our hearts with *love* and we have assurance of salvation. Those "rich in *faith* [are] heirs of the kingdom which He promised to those who *love* Him" (James 2:5).

Faith by itself, without works, is worthless. "You see then that a man is justified by works, and not by *faith* only" (James 2:24). We don't need to appease God. We live to please God. It's *faith* working by *love.*

Paul states: "By grace you have been saved through *faith,* and that not of yourselves; it is the gift of God" (Ephesians 2:8). He quickly adds, "We are His workmanship, created in Christ Jesus for good works" (Ephesians 2:10). We give ourselves fully to Him. He enables us to do His will.

Three different men under very different circumstances ask the same basic question. First is the rich young ruler. "What ... shall I do that I may have eternal life" (Matthew 19:16)?

Jesus responds, "Keep the commandments" (Matthew 19:17).

Next is a lawyer who wants to justify himself. "What shall I do to inherit eternal life" (Luke 10:25)?

Jesus answers with a question, "What is written in the law?" (Luke 10:26).

The lawyer replies correctly: "You shall *love* the Lord ... God with all your heart ... and your neighbor as yourself" (Luke 10:27).

Jesus says, "Do this and you will live" (Luke 10:28).

An earthquake shakes a Philippian jail and the terrified jailer asks, "What must I do to be saved?" (Acts 16:30).

Paul and Silas answer, "Believe on the Lord Jesus Christ, and you will be saved" (Acts 16:31).

One question, three answers. Which is right? All are right! Truly believe on the Lord Jesus Christ and you will *love* God and your neighbor. Loving God and your neighbor, you will keep the commandments!

The rich young ruler learned that to truly obey the commandments, he would need to sell his possessions and give to the poor. The lawyer discovered that loving God and his neighbor meant helping anyone in need. The jailer believed and rejoiced in God. Immediately he and all his family were baptized, washing away the sin in their lives to begin a new life in Christ.

Jesus did not wait for Nicodemus to ask the question. Reading his heart, the Savior said, "Unless one is born again, he cannot see the kingdom of God" (John 3:3). After talking about being born of water and the Spirit, Jesus went on to explain that "Men loved darkness rather than light, because their deeds were evil, … But he who does the truth comes to the light, that his deeds may be clearly seen, that they have been done in God" (John 3:19, 21).

Peter reminds us that whoever "works righteousness is accepted by Him" (Acts 10:35). The *ladder* with eight steps shows how to experience the righteousness of Christ in our lives. It all starts with *faith* and ends with *love.*

I told you how I needed to get on the roof to repair a chimney. Imagine that I go to the garage, haul out my *ladder* with eight steps, and lay it down on the ground. I walk on the *ladder,* but the roof stays out of reach. To get on the roof, I must set up the *ladder* and climb.

Claiming a relationship with Jesus is not enough. I must constantly cling to Him. Walking on the *ladder* gets me nowhere. I must climb. In His Sermon on the Mount, Jesus declared, "Not everyone who says to Me, 'Lord, Lord,' shall enter the kingdom of heaven, but he who does the will of My Father in heaven" (Matthew 7:21).

Alone in a 17-foot fiberglass kayak, I sailed farther off the coast of Bermuda than I intended. I always wanted to do this, but never had time. With a stiff breeze, the tiny craft skimmed over the water. *Haven't had this much excitement for years,* I thought. *It's almost like flying.*

With the shoreline getting farther away every minute, I tightened the sail to go faster. *I'll have one last thrill before heading home.* The thrill came, but not what I hoped for. The boat flipped upside down, dumping me into the Atlantic Ocean. I swam up along the overturned kayak. *I'll turn it right side up, bail out the water, and sail back to shore where I left my family.*

Nothing worked. The more I tried to right the boat, the more frustrated I became. The mast and soaked sail pointed straight down, working against me as I struggled to turn the boat upright. I looked back at Bermuda. *I'm in real trouble. I'll never get this kayak right side up by myself. The wind is blowing me past the island toward the North Atlantic. There's nothing I can do to save myself from this mess.* Suddenly I realized, *I'm totally helpless!*

I climbed up on the overturned kayak and scanned the horizon, hoping to see another boat. Nothing. The sun dropped low on the western horizon. *It's late and all the boats have gone home,* I imagined. *With coral reefs all around, no boat of any size can navigate after dark.*

The last island of Bermuda, St. George's, began to disappear. *Looks like I'll make a nice supper for a hungry shark,* I thought. *If I do make it through the night, I'll be so far out to sea that no one will ever find me. No food, no water, burning sun—I won't last long.*

Shivering in the wind, I slipped back into the warm water. "Lord," I prayed. "My foolishness got me into this. Only you can save me. I need to get back to my wife and daughters, to my church, and the mission. If it's Your will, please send a boat to help me."

I listened. *It's the sound of an engine; I know it is!* The boat rounded the end of the island and headed for the North Shore. *It won't come near me. What can I do?* I considered leaving the kayak and swimming to shore. *No, that won't work. The wind and the tide are taking me past the island. It's miles away. I can never make it.*

Ready to give up I looked toward the north. "A boat!"

As gulls flew overhead, I began waving frantically. A yacht coming home late turned. It headed toward me. "Thank you, Lord. You're answering my prayer."

The skipper pulled his yacht along side. He maneuvered to where they could help me right the kayak. I dropped the sail. The skipper said, "It's late. I don't have time to lose. Where do you need to go?"

"My family is waiting for me on the rocky shore off Crawl Hill," I replied.

"Get in your kayak," he commanded. "Take this rope and hang on. I'll tow you to shore. Use your rudder and stay in the center of my wake."

No time to ask, "Why?" But I soon understood the reason. The boat towing mine created huge waves that could capsize me in seconds. *Clinging to this rope is like putting my faith in Christ,* I thought. *Failing to cling to Jesus, the devil will overwhelm me.*

To hang on while towed in rough water took every ounce of energy I had. It hit me. *I'm saved as long as I hang on to Jesus.* Salvation is sure as long we keep climbing with Christ. Angels stand ready to come to our aid.

A hundred yards off shore, the skipper motioned for me to drop the rope and he cruised on. My family had prayed after they watched me disappear. Now, while the sun slipped below the horizon, they helped me pull the kayak out and carry it up the bank for storage in our garage. No sharks. No miserable night in the open sea. No days dehydrating under a burning sun. Home seemed like heaven.

You and I, lost in the sea of sin, are totally helpless. We can never save ourselves. But God made a plan. He provided a *ladder* to unite us with infinite power. Jacob dreamed about it. Jesus talked about it. Peter points us to the steps we must climb.

On my own I could not get to the yacht for a tow. The skipper came to me. By ourselves, we cannot get to the *lad-*

der. Jesus reaches out to us. Our own efforts cannot save us. Yet we can never be saved without effort. I had to cling to the rope. Jesus declares, "I am the WAY" (John 14:6). We must cling to Him.

Can we really get to heaven? Can we be sure? Because of Jesus' death on the cross, eight simple steps guarantee our salvation—*faith, virtue, science, temperance, patience, piety, fraternity, love.* Jesus is the *ladder.* We can climb to heaven with Him.

You can be sure to get to the top! Christ inspired Peter to write, "For if these things are yours and abound, you will be neither barren nor unfruitful in the knowledge of our Lord Jesus Christ. For he who lacks these things is shortsighted, even to blindness, and has forgotten that he was cleansed from his old sins. Therefore, brethren, be even more diligent to make your calling and election sure, for if you do these things you will never stumble; for so *an entrance will be supplied to you abundantly into the everlasting kingdom of our Lord and Savior Jesus Christ"* (2 Peter 1:8-11).

An entrance will be supplied into heaven if we do these things. What things? "Add to your *faith virtue,* to virtue *science,* to science *temperance,* to temperance *patience,* to patience *piety,* to piety *fraternity,* to fraternity *love"* (2 Peter 1:5-7, author's translation). We don't go around shouting, "I'm saved!" Our hope is in Jesus. Men and women of *faith* mentioned in Hebrews 11 all died without receiving the promise, yet they were assured of a heavenly home.

You and I work on the plan of addition. It's $1 + 1 = 2 + 1 = 3 + 1 = 4 + 1 = 5 + 1 = 6 + 1 = 7 + 1 = 8$. Eight, only eight? No wonder Jesus says, "Without Me, you can do nothing" (John 15:5).

When we climb with Jesus, He works on the plan of multiplication. It's $1 \times 1 = 1 \times 2 = 2 \times 3 = 6 \times 4 = 24 \times 5 = 120 \times 6 = 720 \times 7 = 5,040 \times 8 =$ the amazing sum of 40,320. This is an increase of 504 percent.

Jesus does for us what we can never do for ourselves. His death on the cross paid the penalty for sin. When we repent, He forgives. He sends the Holy Spirit to renew our minds. His grace gives us power to obey. He gives us a desire to do His will. Through *faith* in Him, we receive His righteousness. He will come and take us to heaven.

Take courage! Go forward! Say with Paul, "I press toward the goal for the prize of the upward call of God in Christ Jesus" (Philippians 3: 14). "The peace of God, which surpasses all understanding, will guard your hearts and minds through Christ Jesus" (Philippians 4:7).

The shining *ladder* in Jacob's dream illustrates our relationship with Christ. A *ladder* holds us up while we climb. Jesus provides support when we climb by *faith*, taking the steps of *love*. He is the "author of salvation to all who obey Him" (Hebrews 5:9). Always be "looking to Jesus, the author and finisher of our *faith*" (Hebrews 12:2). Look to the top of the *ladder*. Keep climbing! Soon you will step off into God's eternal kingdom. Because of Jesus, you can be sure!

JESUS is the WAY to heaven,
I will climb with Him.

FAITH in Jesus brings salvation,
Lord increase my faith.

I will live a life of VIRTUE,
Live in purity.

Search God's Word for heaven's SCIENCE.
The *science* of the cross.

I will live a life of TEMPERANCE,
Jesus gives me strength.

I will pray each day for PATIENCE,
Make me more like Christ.
I'll forsake all worldly pleasure,
God gives PIETY.

I will share my faith with others,
God's FRATERNITY.

More and more I LOVE the Savior,
Jesus died for me.

Every round goes higher, higher,
I will meet my God.

Points to Remember

1. Jesus is a *ladder*, not an escalator.
2. Our own efforts will never save us.
3. We cannot be saved without effort.
4. To be saved, we must
   A. By *faith* believe on the Lord Jesus Christ, repent, confess, and forsake sin.
   B. *Love* God with all our heart and our neighbor as our self.
   C. Make *love* the motive for our obedience.
5. Cling to Jesus through Bible study and prayer and climb to the top of the *ladder*.
6. You can overcome "by the blood of the Lamb."
7. Peter shows how you can be absolutely sure to get to heaven (See 2 Peter 1:3-11).
   A. Our *faith* is obtained "by the righteousness of our God and Savior Jesus Christ."
   B. "His divine power has given us all things that pertain to life and godliness."
   C. "You may be partakers of the divine nature, having escaped the corruption that is in the world."
   D. "Add to your *faith*, virtue, science, temperance, patience, piety, fraternity, and *love*."
   E. "Make your calling and election sure."
   F. "If you do these things you will never fall."
   G. *"An entrance will be supplied into the everlasting kingdom of our Lord and Savior Jesus Christ."*

Climb Higher

God Offers Assurance

"Lead me to the rock that is higher than I." (Psalm 61:2).

"He who is guided by ... holy principles will be quick to discern the slightest taint of evil, because he keeps Christ before him as his pattern. His deep regret at the discovery of a wrong act means the prompt correction of every step wherein he has diverged from truth. It means a constant, earnest striving for higher and still higher attainments in the Christian life" (*In Heavenly Places*, 260).

"*Faith, virtue, science, temperance, patience, piety, fraternity, love,* are the rounds of the *ladder*. We are saved by climbing round after round, mounting step after step, to the height of Christ's ideal for us" (Translated from *Los Hechos de Los Apóstoles*, 422. Compare with *The Acts of the Apostles*, 530).

"**As we shall work upon the plan of addition,** by *faith* adding grace to grace, God will work upon the plan of multiplication, and multiply grace and peace unto us" (*The Youth's Instructor*, October 31, 1895).

Look to the Top

"Come, you blessed of My Father, inherit the kingdom prepared for you from the foundation of the world" (Matthew 25:34).

"**Look to the top of the *ladder*.** God is above it. Jesus is this *ladder*. Climb by Him, cling to Him, and ere long you will *step off the ladder into His everlasting kingdom*" (*Testimonies for the Church*, 8:130, 131).

"**He who does not climb the *ladder*** ... has forgotten the claims of God upon him, and that he was to receive forgiveness of sins through obedience to the requirements of God" (*Manuscript Releases*, 19:350, 351).

"**If any of us are finally saved,** it will be by clinging to Jesus as to the rounds of a *ladder* (*Testimonies for the Church*, 5:539).

Assurance for Ladder Climbers

"The work of righteousness will be peace, and the effect of righteousness, quietness and *assurance* forever" (Isaiah 32:17)

"**We need not have a supposed hope,** but an *assurance*. To make our calling and election sure is to follow the Bible plan to closely examine ourselves, to make strict inquiry whether we are indeed converted, whether our minds are drawn out after God and heavenly things, our wills renewed, our whole souls changed" (*Manuscript Releases*, 19:351).

"**No one who perseveringly climbs** the *ladder* will fail of gaining an entrance into the heavenly city" (*Messages to Young People*, 95).

"**Christ is the mystic ladder** uniting the earth with the universe of heaven, and as our *faith* lays hold upon him, we see Him standing as our advocate, *our assurance*, our life" (*Signs of the Times*, Aug. 27, 1895).

Ladder of Sanctification

"**We are saved by climbing round after round of the *ladder*,** looking to Christ, clinging to Christ, mounting step by step to the height of Christ, so that He is made unto us wisdom and *righteousness and sanctification and redemption*" (*Testimonies for the Church*, 6:147).

" **It is my sincere wish for our young people** that they find the true meaning of justification by *faith*, and the perfection of character that will prepare them for eternal life" (*Fundamentals of Christian Education*, 548).

"**Justification can come alone through faith in Christ**" (*Signs of the Times*, August 22, 1892).

"**Provision is made for the repenting sinner**, so that by faith … he may receive forgiveness of sin, find justification, receive adoption into the heavenly family, and become an inheritor of the kingdom of God. Transformation of character is wrought through the operation of the Holy Spirit. … Day by day he is strengthened and renewed by grace, and is enabled more and more perfectly to reflect the character of Christ in righteousness and true holiness" (*Review and Herald*, September 17, 1895).

Climbers with Christ Can Expect Difficulties

"**The gaining of eternal life is no easy thing.** By living *faith* we are to keep on reaching forward, ascending the *ladder* round by round, seeing and taking the necessary steps; and yet we must understand that not one holy thought, not one unselfish act, can be originated in self. It is only through Christ that there can be any virtue in humanity" (*That I May Know Him*, 21).

"**There is round after round of painful ascent;** for our characters must be brought into harmony with the law of God, and every advance step in this direction requires self-denial" (Ellen G. White, *Signs of the Times*, June 26, 1884).

"**The warfare against self** is the greatest battle that was ever fought. The yielding of self, surrendering all to the will of God, requires a struggle; but the soul must submit to God before it can be renewed in holiness" (*Steps to Christ*, 43).

Climbing With Christ Requires Our Cooperation

"Let us hear the conclusion of the whole matter: Fear God, and keep his commandments: for this is the whole duty of man" (Ecclesiastes 12:13, KJV).

"**The conditions of salvation** are ever the same. Life, eternal life, is for all who will obey God's law" (*God's Amazing Grace*, 136).

"**To make God's grace our own**, we must act our part. The Lord does not propose to perform for us either the willing or the doing. His grace is given to work in us to will and to do, but never as a substitute for our effort" (*Messages to Young People*, 147).

"**While we can do nothing without Him,** *we have something to do in connection with Him.* ... We must cling to Christ, climb up by Christ, become laborers together with Him in the saving of our souls" (*That I May Know Him*, 21).

Our Effort Without Christ's Righteousness Will Fail

"Not having my own righteousness, . . . but that which is through faith in Christ" (Philippians 3:9).

"**In this conflict of righteousness against unrighteousness** we can be successful only by divine aid. Our finite will must be brought into submission to the will of the Infinite; the human will must be blended with the divine. This will bring the Holy Spirit to our aid" (*Messages to Young People*, 55).

"**The righteousness** which Christ taught is conformity of heart and life to the revealed will of God. . . . There is no excuse for sinning. A holy temper, a Christlike life, is accessible to every repenting, believing child of God" (*The Desire of Ages*, 310, 311).

"**There are those who attempt to ascend the *ladder* of** Christian progress; but as they advance, they begin to put their trust in the power of man, and soon lose sight of Jesus. ... The result is failure—the loss of all that has been gained" (*The Acts of the Apostles*, 532).

Ladders Support Climbers—Jesus Supports Us

"We may boldly say: 'The Lord is my helper'" (Hebrews 13:6).

"**God ... is watching those who are climbing**, ready, when the grasp relaxes and the steps falter, to send help" (*Messages to Young People*, 95).

"**Christ** ... will never abandon one for whom He has died. Unless His followers choose to leave Him, He will hold them fast" (*The Desire of Ages*, 483).

"**Christ changes the heart**. He abides in your heart by *faith*. You are to maintain this connection with Christ by *faith* and the continual surrender of your will to Him; and so long as you do this, He will work in you to will and to do according to His good pleasure" (*Steps to Christ*, 62, 63).

Righteousness by Faith Is Faith Working by Love

"Has God not chosen the poor of this world to be rich in *faith* and heirs of the kingdom which He promised to those who *love* Him?" (James 2:5).

"**No man can cover his soul** with the garments of Christ's righteousness while practicing known sins, or neglecting known duties. God requires the entire surrender of the heart, before justification can take place; and in order for man to retain justification, there must be continual obedience, through active, living *faith* that works by *love*" (*Selected Messages*, 1:366).

"**As we thus contemplate heavenly themes**, our *faith* and *love* will grow stronger, and our prayers will be more and more acceptable to God, because they will be more and more mixed with *faith* and *love.* They will be intelligent and fervent. There will be more constant confidence in Jesus, and a daily, living experience in His power to save to the uttermost all that come unto God by Him" (*Steps to Christ,* 88).

The true Christian ... is ever climbing, never content with that to which he has attained The more he seeks a knowledge of God, and of Jesus Christ, whom he has sent, the more he desires to reflect the divine image" (*Review and Herald,* October 3, 1899).

w.m.